2⁻

D0399430

At America's Service

How Corporations Can Revolutionize the Way They Treat Their Customers

At America's Service

How Corporations Can Revolutionize the Way They Treat Their Customers

Karl Albrecht

Dow Jones-Irwin
Homewood, Illinois 60430

© DOW JONES-IRWIN, 1988

All rights reserved. No part of this publication may be
reproduced, stored in a retrieval system, or transmitted,
in any form or by any means, electronic, mechanical,
photocopying, recording, or otherwise, without the prior
written permission of the publisher.

This publication is designed to provide accurate and
authoritative information in regard to the subject matter
covered. It is sold with the understanding that the
publisher is not engaged in rendering legal, accounting, or
other professional service. If legal advice or other expert
assistance is required, the services of a competent
professional person should be sought.

*From a Declaration of Principles jointly adopted by a Committee
of the American Bar Association and a Committee of Publishers.*

Acquisitions editor: James Childs
Project editor: Rita McMullen
Production manager: Irene H. Sotiroff
Jacket Design: Studio M
Compositor: Weimer Typesetting Co., Inc.
Typeface: 11/13 Times Roman
Printer: Arcata Graphics/Kingsport

Library of Congress Cataloging-in-Publication Data

Albrecht, Karl.
    At America's service.

    Includes index.
    1. Service industries—United States—Management.
2. Customer relations. 3. United States—Economic
conditions—1981- . I. Title.
HD9981.5.A42 1988   658.8'12   88-3564
ISBN 1-55623-095-8

Printed in the United States of America

1 2 3 4 5 6 7 8 9 0 K 5 4 3 2 1 0 9 8

FOREWORD

J. W. Marriott, Jr.

This is truly the Age of Service. The transition from an economy based on manufacturing to one based on service is one of the most important trends in American life, and certainly in the modern business world. Those of us who are entrusted with the leadership of service businesses bear a special responsibility to our customers, our employees, and our shareholders. The need and the opportunity for achieving excellence in what we do have never been greater.

Yet, there are many challenges in achieving and maintaining the quality standard that our customers have come to want and expect of us. It has never been easy, and it won't get any easier. My father, J. W. Marriott, Sr., often said, "Success is never final." He believed it was harder to stay at the top than to get there. We must set high expectations of our organizations and help people achieve them. And as leaders, we have to live it ourselves every day.

In too many aspects of American life, the idea of *service,* or doing a service job, is considered demeaning and is equated with low status. Too many executives and managers think of service workers as unimportant and replaceable. But in reality, the service people are the most important ones in the organization. Without them there is no product, no sale, and no profit. Indeed, they *are* the product. Service is, and should be, a high calling.

v

We all need to rededicate ourselves every day to giving service employees the leadership, support, and appreciation they need to take care of their customers and to feel that what they're doing is worthwhile. We must do all we can to make our organizations, systems, methods, and policies serve the people who serve the customers. And this applies especially to managers themselves. I am very taken with Karl Albrecht's notion that management is a service and that part of the job of every manager is to support and assist the people who serve the customer. At every opportunity I tell managers in the Marriott Corporation, "Take care of the employees and they'll take care of the customers."

The book you are about to read has an important message—one that has value for every organization in every service industry. Karl Albrecht has done an admirable job of presenting the tools and techniques of service management and showing how any organization can, if its leaders are really determined, become an outstanding service performer. With his clear and highly readable explanation of exciting new ideas, Karl has made a major contribution to contemporary management thinking.

I urge all executives and managers to read this book carefully, reflect on its message, and apply its principles in their organizations.

Contents

Problems.   Organizational Arthritis.   Middle Management
Inertia.   Conflicted Value Systems.   Misaligned
Incentives.   Gaming.   Headquarters-Field Conflict.

CHAPTER 1

THE SERVICE REVOLUTION

There are no such things as service industries. There are only industries whose service components are greater or less than those of other industries. Everybody is in service.
—*Theodore Levitt*
Editor, Harvard Business Review

THE SERVICE REVOLUTION GATHERS STEAM

The service revolution in American business is well underway and gathering steam. Since publication of *Service America!: Doing Business in the New Economy* in 1985, many companies have adopted the service management model as their primary driving idea for competing in the service marketplace. Many more are trying to lift their games by various means and become more effective at delivering their service products. More and more advertising campaigns are zeroing in on service as the competitive factor. The war is on in earnest.

Browse through the adverts in almost any slick magazine these days—*The New Yorker, Time, Business Week, US News & World Report,* or any of the in-flight magazines you find in the seat-pocket of the airplane—and you see a strong shift in orientation toward a service promise. Major airline companies that have been notorious for poor service are trying to convince prospective customers that they have changed their ways. Hotel chains, hospital companies, financial services companies, banks, telecommunications companies, and a host of others are trying to position themselves competitively on service quality.

The demand for training products and information on service management is expanding rapidly. Training programs on customer service are back in vogue. Seminar companies offer service management seminars, and many publishers of training media are dusting off their customer service products and putting them at the top of the list again. Even university extensions, usually the last institutions to join a new trend, offer courses in "achieving service excellence."

The list of major corporations adopting the service management model reads like the "Who's Who" of the Fortune 500. *Service America!* is required reading for the more than 500 general managers of Sheraton hotels. Marriott hotel managers, Marriott In-Flite division catering managers, and managers of Marriott Host airport restaurants and gift shops use the book as their handbook for service management.

Denny's restaurants use service management as the foundation of their Total Guest Satisfaction program. Boston Edison, one of the oldest electric utility companies in the country, adopted service management as its model for organization renewal, around the focus of total customer service.

Shearson Lehman Hutton, the giant brokerage firm, uses service management principles to sharpen its market position in the highly competitive investment industry. Merrill Lynch uses the book and the film "Service Management" to help several thousand employees understand their internal service roles.

While my previous coauthor Ron Zemke and I are flattered by those who consider *Service America!* the new manifesto for the management of service, we are also concerned lest too many people mistake service management for the latest fad. Making a service business truly customer driven turns out to be very challenging, as many executives are discovering. It does not come cheaply, easily, or without effort. It will never be stylish as an easy fix.

My American approach to service management has evolved quite a bit from its origins as a takeoff from the Scandinavian Airlines idea. The issues, problems, and pitfalls inherent in its implementation are now much better understood. It is now possible, I believe, to provide a clearer perspective on implementation of a wall-to-wall service management program.

I have observed and worked with a variety of service businesses and seen firsthand the hurdles they have had to clear to make the service philosophy a way of life. I believe there is much more now to share.

WHAT WE'VE LEARNED ABOUT SERVICE

Ron Zemke and I were asked recently to share with a group of training officers and organization development people from various firms the 10 lessons we had learned about service and service management during the time we have been working with the concept. Here are the items we nominated as our most important realizations.

1. *Service has more economic impact than we thought and is worse than we imagined.* Continuing customer research shows that many service firms are paying a terribly high price in the "opportunity cost" of lost business due to mediocre service. In many industries, both market share and market volume are there for the taking by the firms that can gain a truly differentiated position around service excellence.

2. *Most service organizations are in the defensive mode with respect to quality.* The customer service department remains, for the majority of service businesses, the only token of commitment to satisfying customer needs. In most companies, the CS department is the group of people whose job it is to get trounced by the customer when the rest of the organization fouls things up. Few firms are truly proactive with respect to customer satisfaction and making amends for disservice events. The simple apology is still, by and large, a lost art in the world of business.

3. *Management must see the profit impact of service in order to take it seriously.* Organizations typically start to turn on only when their senior management groups "grok" (in the words of science fiction writer Robert Heinlein) the idea that there is money to be made in doing right by the customer.

4. *The longer you're in a service business, the greater the odds you don't understand your customer.* In case after case, research into customer perceptions reveals hidden concerns, priorities, and feelings that point toward a reconceptualization of the service product and a clearer positioning strategy for the service in its marketplace.

5. *A service product is profoundly different from a physical product.* A service is a psychological and largely personal outcome, whereas a physical product is usually "impersonal" in its impact on the customer. Most executives and managers in service businesses are still trying to depersonalize the product

and run their organizations with thing-oriented philosophies and practices.

6. *Managers do not control the quality of the product when the product is a service.* Quality control changes drastically when the product is an interaction rather than a thing. The quality of the service product is in a precarious state—it is in the hands of the service workers who "produce" and deliver it. Managers can affect the quality of service only indirectly, by inspiring and motivating the people at the front line. Many of those managers don't realize this yet.

7. *Service improvement starts at the top; managers must "walk their talk."* Research and practical experience show that a universal commitment to quality service does not spontaneously ignite in organizations. It must originate from the center of influence, which is usually at the top of the pyramid. If senior management believes in service, there is a chance the idea can become contagious. If they don't really believe in it, it will go nowhere fast, regardless of what they say.

8. *Management practice will have to evolve from a manufacturing orientation to a moments-of-truth orientation to meet the demands of competition.* We are at the beginning of an era that will see the demise of the General Motors model of management, with its tool-and-task orientation, and the evolution of a new motif that will revolve around outcomes instead of activities. This will probably be a long, slow process, taking at least a decade to get into full swing. The early thought leaders will take the lumps for the learning process, but they may reap significant rewards in market performance and organizational productivity.

9. *Your employees are your first market; you have to sell them on the service idea or they will never sell it to your customers.* The way your people feel about themselves and their jobs will always affect their interactions with the customers. If they believe in giving the best service they possibly can, it will show. If you haven't sold them, that will show too. And they do need to be sold in most cases, or at the very least, not unsold.

10. *Systems are often the enemies of service.* Many of the problems of poor or mediocre service originate in systems, procedures, policies, rules and regulations, and organizational craziness. Too often, we blame the frontline people for poor service, when the real problem is systems that don't work or make sense. If you aren't willing to rethink the systems, you're asking them to run the race with only one shoe.

Of course, we've learned a great deal more than these 10 things, but they do serve as jumping-off points for discussion about how to make the service revolution happen in the firm.

THE SERVICE 500

One of the many indications of the service revolution is that business analysts are beginning to treat service businesses as a clearly differentiated industrial category, worthy of statistical tracking and monitoring. *Fortune* magazine now publishes reports on The Service 500 as well as on the classic Fortune 500 the publication has been following for many years.

More than three quarters of all jobs created in the United States during the last decade have been in service industries. The U.S. Bureau of Labor Statistics estimates the trend will continue at about that pace for some time. A majority of new business start-ups are service or service-related businesses.

Fortune's figures tell an interesting story of growth and profitability. While the 500 largest manufacturing companies experienced an aggregate decline in profits of 6.6 percent in 1986, the service 500 showed an increase of 8 percent.

Most of the financial success stories among the largest and most diversified service firms center on natural advantages conferred on them by declining interest rates, lower oil prices, and low inflation rates. Many of the mega-service firms are in the financial services business, dealing more in "back-room" services rather than frontline personal interaction services. At this stage, most of the thinking in these industries equates success with environmental factors and secondarily with marketing moves, rather than with direct value-for-the-dollar service to the customer.

Fortune's list includes eight service industry categories:

1. Commercial banking companies.
2. Diversified financial companies.
3. Diversified service companies.

4. Life insurance companies.
5. Retailing.
6. Savings institutions.
7. Transportation.
8. Utilities.

This particular division of categories doesn't necessarily make the most sense, but it is a start. The category of diversified services seems to be a catch-all, or miscellaneous, category that includes leisure and travel, construction, hospitals and health care, real estate, and a variety of others.

It might make more sense to use more focused categories that give a clearer differentiation for market analysis, but we must bear in mind that *Fortune* is a financially oriented publication and its categories reflect the fact that its researchers think in terms of balance sheets and income statements rather than products, markets, and customers.

In any case, it is clear that the service revolution is continuing, as the shift in the American industrial base proceeds toward more and more of a service economy. Similarly, virtually all of the other postindustrial nations are experiencing much the same shift, in differing degrees and at differing stages. Even China, which has a long way to go to become anything like a consumerist society, has accepted and embraced the efforts of western service corporations like Sheraton to set up tourist services for the growing market. A major milestone: Kentucky Fried Chicken, a subsidiary of Pepsico, has been allowed to set up the first fast-food restaurant in Beijing. The verdict: according to the Chinese, "We like it very much."

IS GOVERNMENT A SERVICE?

C. Northcote Parkinson, the acerbic British writer and creator of the famous Parkinson's Law, observed, "If there's anything a public servant hates to do, it's something for the public."

Some of the more cynical members of the public refer to the term *government service* as an *oxymoron,* which semanticists define as the juxtaposition of two or more contradictory meanings, like jumbo shrimp, military intelligence (according to Groucho Marx), and postal service.

The early American humorist Will Rogers used to admonish people, "Just be glad you're not getting all the government you're paying for."

It's a shame that government agencies in general have such a poor image for service, but most of them have earned it. Why is it that, in virtually all Western nations, whose citizens basically consider government to be a service, the prevailing image of government organizations and government employees is one of indifference, ineffectiveness, and inefficiency? Why do civil servants have the image of being lazy, unmotivated, indifferent to the needs of the public, and concerned only with job security?

Case in Point: On my desk is a form letter from a federal agency. It reads:

Dear Customer: (*Good start.*)

We are returning your remittance, which we received with insufficient information to process it. Because of the high volume of correspondence that we receive daily, we cannot match remittances and orders mailed to us separately. (*Translation: We lost your order form.*)

Please resubmit your payment with all pertinent information concerning your request. Address your correspondence with remittance to, etc.

We apologize for any inconvenience this may have caused you. (*Nice touch.*)

The language of the letter—which arrived three weeks after the order was sent—betrays a bureaucratic, authoritarian mindset. Terms like *remittance, correspondence, resubmit,* and *request* all suggest that the writer sees the agency as in an authority position rather than a customer-service position. The citizen is a "requester," not a customer. The message is: you have misbehaved. If you will learn to behave properly and follow our rules, we will give you what you want. Otherwise, take your money and shove it.

Maybe I'm being a bit harsh, but this incident is one of many thousands that occur daily when people interact with city, county, state, and federal agencies. Many government people, consciously or unconsciously, perceive themselves as in positions of bureaucratic influence over the public rather than at the disposal of the public.

In 1976, when the state of California passed its controversial Proposition 13 legislation, which limited the levels of local property taxes and forced budget cuts among local government agencies, bureaucrats in many areas retaliated immediately. They began cutting out small but highly visible services, so the inconsiderate voters would feel the consequences of their ballot-box decisions. In very few instances did government leaders rally their people together and say, "Let's see what we can do to give the highest possible level of service to the public under the constraints of this new policy of austerity."

Not long ago, I called the Australian consulate in Los Angeles to work out a tricky commercial visa application that was required for me to present a series of seminars in Australia. The Australian woman who answered the telephone—on each of the dozen or so occasions I called—was impolite to the point of rudeness. She expressed no sympathy for the short time constraints I was dealing with and became belligerent when I gently reminded her that her job was to help me get the visa, not prevent me from getting it. Other departments in the consulate reacted in ways ranging from indifferent to irritable, when I could get them to answer their telephones.

The situation seemed all the more grotesque because I was planning to travel to that country to teach service management. At that time, the Australian Tourist Board was airing commercials on American television, starring actor Paul Hogan of *Crocodile Dundee* fame, inviting Americans to come and sample the relaxed friendliness and hospitality down under, while this woman was doing her best to talk them out of it.

The reason government "service" is generally so poor, with a few notable exceptions, is very simple: *it isn't necessary* for government entities to give good service. No survival factor operates in the thinking of government managers, such as there is for those in charge of commercial enterprises. If a hotel gives lousy service, the customer votes with his or her money and takes the patronage elsewhere. But seldom does a government organization, regardless of its charter, have any compelling reason to serve. In most cases, there isn't any elsewhere.

When you consider the far-reaching consequences of this permanent guarantee of existence, this lack of any predatory force in the organization's environment that might threaten its survival, you can understand how completely this motif of indifference penetrates all the nooks and crannies of so many government organizations. It becomes an all-pervading cultural norm, to which all but the most self-motivated and idealistic individuals eventually succumb. Getting a government organization to be really customer driven and service oriented is *really* like teaching an elephant to dance.

Yet, the opportunities—and the potential payoffs—for service-oriented government operations are enormous. Try to picture this: government agencies at all levels, all around the country, operating as if they were in existence to serve. Government executives, middle managers, and supervisors telling their people every day, "Our job is to provide the highest quality service we possibly can." It's an exciting prospect, however quixotic it may seem.

I am occasionally asked: what does it take for a government organization to become really service oriented? Who or what can supply the incentive?

I always answer: *somebody in charge has to care*. Because the government organization typically has no competitive wolves at its heels, it has no internalized compulsion to make a hit with its customers. Therefore, the only way to wake it up and put it on the right track is for the person in charge to become obsessed with the idea of service and service management and to take concerted, aggressive, long-term action to transform its culture.

A government executive will do this only if his or her personal value system provides a compelling motive for action. And that is very rare, indeed.

THE STATE OF SERVICE TODAY

A customer walked up to the airline ticket counter and said, "I'd like to fly from here to Chicago; but I'd like you to send this suitcase to Toronto and this one to Washington." The ticket agent looked at her incredulously and replied, "I'm sorry, ma'am, we can't do that." The customer said, "Why not? You did it last week!"

One of the questions posed to me most frequently after speeches to management groups is, "What happens when everybody is doing service management? What will be the advantage when all of our competitors are also service driven?" The implied question is, "Won't we lose any competitive advantage we might have gained by being a leader in the revolution?"

My standard answer is: there is absolutely no risk of that happening. At most, 10 to 15 percent of companies in any one industry will be willing to make the kind of all-out commitment necessary to become really service driven in their operations.

When I say there is a service revolution underway, I don't mean to imply that all service businesses are engaged in it. Some people lead the revolution, some are led, and some sleep through it. It's probably fair to say that, at present, service businesses fall into five categories in terms of the degree of commitment they display to service quality. These five levels are:

1. *Going out of business.* These firms are so out of touch with their customers that they are on the way down the tubes; some know it, some don't.

2. *Dogged pursuit of mediocrity.* These firms are probably in business to stay, but service quality is not part of their thinking. Some fairly major companies fall into this category, including a number of airlines. Many government agencies operate at Level 2, largely because they lack a profit imperative.

3. *Present and accounted for.* These firms know they are in the service business and tend to have an innate respect for doing at least the basics. However, most of them enjoy only what marketing theorists call a "natural market share," i.e., the share of the market they're entitled to by virtue of showing up. Service quality doesn't play a major part in their strategic positioning. Many, if not most, banks fall into this category, as well as many retail chains and quite a few hotels.

4. *Making a serious effort.* These firms are on the move, and they are usually working hard to find ways to make service a competitive weapon. This is the level at which service management makes sense as an organizational "driving idea." A number of major firms as well as many smaller ones are working at, arriving at, or passing through this level. A great deal of innovation, risk-taking, and rethinking of customer image and organizational focus goes on here.

5. *Service as an art form.* These are the legendary firms in the service business—those very few that have become household names and market leaders because of their obsessive, unrelenting commitment at all levels to the doctrine of maximum positive customer impact. These are the Marriotts, the Disneys, the Nordstrom department stores, the IBMs (in the old days), and a number of smaller firms that are legends in their corners of the world. World-class restaurants and hotels and a very few cruise ships fit into this category. The mission of management in these companies is to preserve and refine the image of outstanding service. Figure 1–1 illustrates these levels of service quality with respect to competitive impact.

Many of the companies that are hoping to make service their competitive edge factor will not succeed, simply because they won't be able to raise their levels of service quality high enough to

FIGURE 1–1
Levels of Service Quality

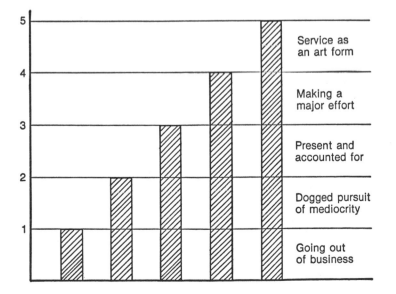

make a significant difference. My definition of service excellence, from the standpoint of competitive positioning is:

> **Service excellence: A level of service quality, compared to your competitors, that is high enough in the eyes of your customers that it enables you to charge a higher price for your service product, gain an unnaturally large market share, and/or enjoy a higher profit margin than your competitors.**

To enjoy any or all of these advantages you must have, in my opinion, a Level 5 quality of service in the eyes of the customer. Simply trying hard won't do it. Advertising campaigns won't do it. Exhorting the employees to love the customer won't do it. The only thing that will do it is to deliver a superior service product that wins in the marketplace.

From the standpoint of competitive strength, a company with a Level 1 or Level 2 service product won't be in the running, even if it manages to stay in business. A Level 3 company can expect to get its basic piece of the turf. If there are N competitors in the field, it can expect about one Nth of the market, more or less. Service leadership is all about *unnatural* market share, i.e., getting a piece of somebody else's pie. And that takes a well-marketed, superior product.

Those who sample public opinion on a regular basis report that the general perception of service quality in most Western countries is pretty dismal. Rightly or wrongly, T. C. Mits [better known as "The Celebrated Man (or Woman) in the Street"] believes he is getting a bum deal for his money from most service businesses. Even allowing for the fact that most people like to hear themselves complain, the evidence suggests most people believe service quality in general has a long way to go.

There seems to be growing exasperation in all quarters with service and service establishments, and the increasing tide of magazine articles and newspaper editorials bears witness to the mood of the times.

News Item: A group of angry airline passengers rioted at the Miami airport recently after Eastern Airlines gate agents announced the cancellation of their flight. Eastern brought in a replacement airplane, but its smaller capacity could accommodate only about half of the passengers. The rest found themselves facing the prospect of being stranded overnight in the airport. Eastern representatives called in city police to control the disturbance, which incensed the customers all the more. The resulting melee led to several arrests, mass confusion, and a customer-service nightmare for the airline.

This incident came at a time when the collective image of the major American airline companies was near an all-time low. It was so low, in fact, that Congress had taken the unprecedented initiative to investigate the low levels of service in the airline industry, in consideration of possible regulations requiring airline companies to measure and publicize their service records.

A glance at some typical articles conveys a sense of the exasperation and irritation many people are feeling. None other than *Time* magazine devoted an extensive cover story to what it considered the sad state of service in America. Titled "Why Is Service So Bad?" it backhanded one industry after another for failing to look after the quality of the customer's experience. The article was triggered by a string of customer experiences of a *Time* senior editor who had just returned from living in Japan. He was shocked to see the contrast between the highly deferential style of service in that country and the indifferent—and often rude—service he found in his native country.

Money magazine recently carried an article titled, "The Six Rudest Restaurants in America." It detailed a number of characteristically negative experiences customers had with "restaurants noted for their h'ordeals rather than their hors d'oeuvres." These included some of the swankiest of the swank: the Ivy in Beverly Hills, Mortimer's in Manhattan, Spago in West Hollywood, K-Paul's in New Orleans, Caffe Sport in San Francisco, and AV Ristorante in Washington, D.C.

The author, Michelle Williams, identified the most common insults to customers: grossly overbooking reservations; holding the better tables for favorite customers; maitre d's who could suddenly materialize a good table in exchange for a heavy tip; treating customers with attitudes bordering on arrogance; and downright rudeness. More than one customer Williams interviewed said the same thing: "They acted like we should feel privileged to eat there." Some of these establishments charged upwards of $75 to $100 for a two-person dinner.

Often when browsing through a local newspaper, I find an editorial commenting on the need for service businesses to wise up and rethink their product. Many are doing exactly that, but many more are not.

THE SEVEN SINS OF SERVICE

With as many service businesses as there are today, and with the service revolution well underway, one would think almost all businesses would pay close attention to the quality of their service. Yet that is far from true. In a majority of service businesses, mediocrity is the norm. Many of them get by with little or no real attention to the customer's experience. They leave the matter of quality largely to chance, and as a consequence they get mediocre quality. It is a simple fact that, in business as well as in life:

The pursuit of mediocrity is always successful.

If you look at the things we service consumers complain about, you can see that there are only a few things that really bug us about the services we try to buy. The same few themes appear over and over. If you examine the complaints customers make to, about, or against service businesses—perhaps your business, as well—you will see they tend to fall into a few basic categories.

After studying a lot of information on customer dissatisfaction, I identified seven categories of complaint factors, which I call the seven sins of service.

FIGURE 1–2
The Seven Sins of Service

1. **Apathy**
2. **Brush-Off**
3. **Coldness**
4. **Condescension**
5. **Robotism**
6. **Rule Book**
7. **Runaround**

1. *Apathy:* A just-don't-give-a-damn attitude on the part of the customer-contact person, or an impression conveyed to the customer expressed in terms of what comedian George Carlin describes as "DILLIGAD," or, "Do I Look Like I Give a Damn?" Many counter-service people get this way when they get bored with their jobs and nobody is reminding them that their jobs are to serve rather than stand behind the counter.

2. *Brush-Off:* Trying to get rid of the customer by brushing off his or her need or problem; trying to "slam dunk" the customer with some standard procedure that doesn't solve the problem but lets the service person off the hook for doing anything special. An example is the department store clerk who is standing around waiting for the end of the shift who says, "This isn't my department," when a customer asks for help in finding something.

3. *Coldness:* A kind of chilly hostility, curtness, unfriendliness, inconsiderateness, or impatience with the customer that says, "You're a nuisance; please go away." It still amazes me to find that so many restaurants carefully select the most moody, depressed, hostile person they can find for the hostess-cashier job, making sure the customer's first and last moments of truth are good ones.

4. *Condescension:* Treating the customer with a patronizing attitude, such as many health-care people do. They call the doctor "*Doctor* Jones," but they call you by your first name and talk to you like you're four years old. They don't think you're qualified to know what your blood pressure is—the doctor will take care of everything.

5. *Robotism:* "Thank-you-have-a-nice-day-NEXT." The fully mechanized worker puts every customer through the same program with the same standard motions and slogans, and with no trace of warmth or individuality. A variant of this is the smiling robot who gives you a permanent "star" smile, but you can tell nobody's home upstairs.

6. *Rule Book:* Putting the organizational rules above customer satisfaction, with no discretion on the part of the service person to make exceptions or use common sense. Banks are famous for this; they usually do everything possible to eliminate all traces of human thought and judgment, with the result that no one is authorized to think. Any customer problem with more than one moving part confounds their system.

7. *Runaround:* "Sorry, you'll have to call (see) so-and-so. We don't handle that here." Airline people have made this into an art; the ticket agent tells you the gate people will take care of it, and the gate people tell you to see the ticket agent when you get to your destination, and the agent at your destination tells you to have your travel agent take care of it.

Life has only so many plots, and if you observe long enough you'll see almost all of them acted out sooner or later. For a personal exercise, pay attention to the service episodes you experience for about a week, and see how many times you get less than satisfactory service. When you do, see which of the seven sins of service you've been subjected to.

If you manage or work with service people, discuss these seven sins of service with them and see what you and they can do to make sure they are not guilty of them.

THE BATTLE OF SLOGANS

We appear to be headed into an interesting period in business over the next several years, especially regarding service as a competitive factor. I characterize this phase as the "battle of slogans." It seems that every service company has to have a slogan or a nifty buzz-phrase to put on the lapel buttons it sticks on its employees. More and more advertisements for service businesses of all kinds brag about how much they care about the customer, how they go all out to please the customer, and how eager their people are to give great service.

As has been the case in advertising for many years, any connection between the claim and the reality tends to be a statistical coincidence. When a firm shows its customers a jarring contradiction between the claim of being service oriented and the reality the customer experiences, chances are the executives have taken a simpleminded approach to customer service. If the concept is simpleminded, so will be the organization's approaches to customer satisfaction.

An amusing story circulated widely in K mart Corporation, one of the largest department store chains in the United States. According to the story, K mart executives wanted all cashiers to say to the customers as they left, "Thank You for Shopping at K mart." They hammered and hammered on this slogan and the need for everybody to say it. They even reduced it to a kind of code— TYFSAK. TYFSAK became a shorthand for saying the slogan. In one instance, a supervisor was training a new cashier. He was standing behind her in the checkout booth, advising her on the various steps in the process. As she was about to hand the change and receipt to the customer, the supervisor whispered to her, "Don't forget to say TYFSAK." A bit confused, she looked at the customer and said, "TYFSAK." The customer, of course, was completely baffled.

Probably at least 50 percent of top executives and senior managers mistake the concept of service leadership for a slogan approach. Somehow they seem to believe (they really do) that all it takes is to round up everybody and give them a dose of "customer service." Or better yet, if the marketing department can come up with a nifty slogan or an ad campaign, it won't even be necessary to put the lapel buttons on the employees or to send them through the smile training courses.

Abraham Lincoln had a favorite riddle he liked to spring on people. He used to ask, "How many legs does a dog have, if you call the tail a leg?" When the unsuspecting respondent would answer, "Five," Lincoln would chastise, "No—he has four. Calling his tail a leg doesn't make it a leg." And calling mediocre service excellent doesn't make it excellent.

We will probably go through a phase in which just about every company will have a customer service promise in its advertising, whether its operation delivers on that promise or not. When we reach that point, customers will be right back where they started— making their judgments on the actual quality of service as they perceive it. Sloganism will only beget an even greater level of customer cynicism and probably not much else.

The advice I usually give to executives who are just getting excited about service excellence and trying to launch service-quality initiatives in their organizations is:

If you can't deliver quality, don't advertise quality.

Years ago I heard a wonderful little poem that illustrates the dangers of advertising something you can't deliver. I've attempted unsuccessfully to find the name of the author. Apparently it has passed along from person to person for many years, and the name has been lost. I pass it along again, with recognition and gratitude to the anonymous poet:

It Pays to Advertise?
A tiger met a lion as they drank beside the pool.
"Tell me," said the tiger, "Why you're always roaring like a fool."
"It's not so foolish," said the lion with a twinkle in his eyes.
"They call me King of Beasts; it pays to advertise."
A little rabbit overheard, and ran home like a streak.
He thought he'd try the lion's plan but his roar was just a squeak.
And a hungry fox that morning had his breakfast in the woods;
The moral: it does *not* pay to advertise unless you have the goods.

–Anonymous

IT'S NO EASY WALK

So here we are, four years after the importation of the basic idea of service management into the United States and two and one-half years after the publication of *Service America!* Where are we, what do we know, and what are the prospects for managing service? I think we know approximately the following:

1. Service is becoming more and more a competitive factor.
2. Quality service translates into profit in most industries.
3. Service is currently unmanaged in most cases.
4. There are only a few really excellent service companies.
5. Enormous competitive opportunities exist in most industries.
6. Becoming service oriented is much tougher than we thought.
7. We know ways that work and ways that won't work.

One impressive thing I and many executives have learned is that teaching the elephant to dance is a big job. I have had the fortunate opportunity to watch many companies try to come to terms with the matter of service competitiveness, and in almost every case the job was bigger than they bargained for.

Some executives have responded to the unexpected difficulty by backing off—consciously or unconsciously—and reverting to the conventional focus on resource control and bottom line performance. Some have become terribly disillusioned. Others have redoubled their determination and set out on aggressive, ambitious programs to make service focus a reality, whatever it takes.

These are exciting times. The challenge is there; the opportunity is there. It's not easy picking by any means, but that drawback has an upside. If you and your company can move quickly to make service quality the driving idea for your business, you will catch most of the players in your competitive field napping. Those who decide to make the investment in time, money, executive energy, and organizational transformation will, in my opinion, be able to gain the competitive high ground if they pull if off.

That's what the rest of this book is about—how to pull it off. Although I don't have the absolute last word on how to solve all the problems of service quality, I have observed a number of successes and failures over several years and learned what works and what doesn't. In the following pages, I will describe and explain the most common pitfalls companies encounter in trying to become service driven. I will pinpoint the most common mistakes executives make in implementing service quality programs and offer a framework for the kind of wall-to-wall effort that is necessary to create and maintain a service culture that can enable the company to make a difference in its marketplace.

CHAPTER 2

SERVICE MANAGEMENT

The only thing that counts is a satisfied customer.
—Jan Carlzon
President, Scandinavian Airlines

WHAT IS SERVICE MANAGEMENT?

Service management has quickly become a popular term in the United States. It is a comfortable and useful handle for the management philosophy that lies behind total service excellence. Most people quickly grasp the frame of reference and the thought process behind it, but some feel the need for a concise, verbally compact statement of definition. Here is the definition I usually offer when asked:

> **Service management is a total organizational approach that makes quality of service, as perceived by the customer, the number one driving force for the operation of the business.**

This definition has several immediate implications that make service management very different from traditional approaches to customer service. It is a transformational concept in my view. It goes far beyond the conventional practices that companies have typically applied to operate in service industries. It was this global character of the Scandinavian concept of managing service that captured my attention when I first discovered it—quite by accident—in Denmark.

After my brief exposure to the Scandinavian idea, I began to realize that American management approaches to service typically involved two basic lines of action, both of which seemed terribly limited in their effectiveness. The first, and most common, is the "customer service department." Most department stores, hospitals, hotels, airlines, and so on will have some person or department designated to handle customer problems. But the customer service department is typically the complaint department and seldom anything else. That is, the unit usually makes little or no contribution until a dissatisfied customer presents a problem.

In the Scandinavian view, having a customer service department may not be a good thing. The mere existence of such a group sends an implied message to everyone else in the organization that says, "Somebody is taking care of the customer, so you can just go about your job and not worry about it."

The service management philosophy suggests that everybody has a part to play in making sure things turn out right for the customer. Certainly anyone who is in direct contact with the customer should feel responsible to see things from the customer's point of view and to do whatever is possible to satisfy the need. But everyone else needs to have the customer in the back of his or her mind also. Under the service management philosophy, the whole organization should operate like one big customer service department.

The other approach we typically take in America is a knee-jerk management reaction to rising levels of customer complaints. When the stack of complaint letters on the president's desk gets too high, he pounds his fist and calls for action. Characteristically, whichever executive is charged with solving these kinds of problems will direct that there be customer service training. They round up the usual suspects—the contact-level employees—and put them all through "smile training" courses. The employees sit through seminars on how to smile, how to be nice, and how to stroke the customers. Often they come out of the classes feeling put down and chastised, as if they have been punished and don't know why.

This approach seems to start with the assumption that the frontline people are the problem—that they are defective in some way and must be fixed. More often than not, however, the problem originates in the lack of any kind of quality commitment or service focus on the part of the organization's management. The employees are simply conforming to the expectations communicated to them. After the employees have gone through the psychological car wash and have been re-adjusted, managers can go back to their other concerns feeling confident that they have done something about the customer service problem. Smile training may have a short-term energizing effect and can sometimes produce better reactions from the customers. But it seldom produces lasting results if the culture is not there to support and sustain the new employee behavior.

The service management approach starts on a much more fundamental level than either of the two approaches just described. It seeks to build a *service culture* that makes excellent service to the customer a recognized mission for everyone in the organization, including the managers. It begins with the responsibility of top management to define the business mission and to specify the strategy needed to make service quality the key to the operation of the business. Once managers at all levels are ready to understand, support, and contribute to the service mission, they will begin doing the right things to help the frontline people take care of the customers. Instead of flogging the employees for poor service, managers must provide the leadership and support they need to help them do an outstanding job.

Our mission in this book is to paint a definitive picture of service management as an overall approach, a philosophy, a management model, and a set of methods and tools that can transform an organization into a service-oriented, customer-driven business. If we can do that, we will automatically be doing the right things for the employees and for the customers. Our training programs will reflect the commitment to service excellence without insulting the employees' intelligence, and our organizational structures will be resourceful to both the employees and the customers.

A NEW WAY OF THINKING

Service management, as a management model and a philosophy, is catching the attention of executives in many service businesses. It offers a unifying framework for thinking about the market, the customer, the product, and the organization. For the first time, leaders of service organizations have a way to get everyone in the organization on the same road.

But adopting the service management philosophy sooner or later forces them to reexamine some of their most basic assumptions, beliefs, and thinking habits. Service management is one of those models that "stays for dinner." It has side effects, both intellectual and psychological. For service management to work effectively, executives need to turn their world views around and look at some old things in some new ways. Forcing this paradigm expansion to happen is one of the great unseen values of the philosophy.

During the several years I have been evolving and working with the American version of service management, I've talked with many executives from different kinds of service businesses. In the majority of these conversations, I have heard—and seen—the process of executives reforming their frames of reference. They are coming to see the service product as fundamentally different, in some very important ways, from a conventional manufactured product. This new way of looking at the organization's product profoundly alters their ways of thinking about their customers, their organizations, and their jobs as managers.

Service management suggests a new urgency with respect to the view of the customer. In a service business, satisfied customers are assets. If you want to buy a service business such as a medical practice, a restaurant, or an insurance brokerage, you will have to pay more than the value of the equipment and the facilities. There is equity in customer satisfaction. If the business is in decline and losing customers, you will have to pay less than if it has a strong base of customer loyalty and repeat business. The future purchases of the customers have a certain present value as part of the intangible equity of the business.

Jan Carlzon, president of Scandinavian Airlines, is particularly blunt about it. He says, "Look at our balance sheet. On the asset side, you can still see so-and-so many aircraft worth so-and-so many billions. But it's wrong; we are fooling ourselves. What we should put on the asset side is, last year SAS carried so-and-so many happy passengers. Because that's the only asset we've got—people who are happy with our service and are willing to come back and pay for it once again."

It makes sense to think of the customers as an *appreciating asset* of the business. An appreciating asset is one that grows in value over time, and that's exactly what happens if customer satisfaction and customer loyalty are increasing over time. Managers in many service businesses need to start thinking in terms of the lifetime income stream available from any one customer. In banking, for instance, a teenager opens his or her first checking account. Most banks typically look upon this as an isolated sales event, having no significance beyond the revenue generated by the service charges and the income on the funds.

But this teenager is not an isolated event in customer land. He or she is at the start of a long life as a consumer of financial services. When it comes time to finance a car, borrow money for college, finance another car, buy furniture for the first household, finance a home, or remodel a home, is the bank there making the sale? Usually it is not. Most people do business with banks more or less at random because so few banks are organized and oriented to market according to a customer-life-cycle point of view.

The same reasoning applies in virtually every service business. This is why it makes so little sense to deal with the customer in strict, unbending ways that interfere with satisfaction and undermine loyalty. The customer complaint, the request for a refund or exchange, the special favor, all take on a much bigger significance when seen in light of the customer as a long-term appreciating asset. Each individual contact with the customer is an important part of the service product and plays a major role in building the value of that customer asset.

This view of the customer, this redefinition of the product, and this rethinking of what the company is in business to do is the starting point for the whole philosophy of management of a service establishment. This brings us to the concept of moments of truth.

MOMENTS OF TRUTH: WHEN YOUR "PRODUCT" IS A SERVICE

Albert Einstein, one of our greatest scientists and philosophers, once described his view on reality by saying, "God is in the details." He believed that nothing at the microscopic level of existence was left to chance; everything followed a design. We can paraphrase Einstein for our purposes: quality of service is in the details. That is, the relationship between the service provider and the service buyers exists at many individual points of contact.

This fact makes a service product fundamentally and unavoidably different from a hard physical product, especially with respect to quality assurance. If you are manufacturing a physical product like an automobile or a television set, you can control the quality of the product by doing all of the manufacturing in one place and inspecting the products as they come off the manufacturing line. But this is not the case with services, like opening bank accounts or administering medications. A service is "manufactured" at the instant of delivery, and in most cases there are many points of delivery, not just one.

In a retail convenience store chain, for instance, thousands of people at many locations produce and deliver the service product. You can manufacture all of the physical products they sell at one central location, but you cannot manufacture their interactions with your customers at one central location. They must do the manufacturing, moment by moment, many thousands of times every day.

This means the traditional methods of quality assurance—centralization and inspection—are no longer valid. We need a new conceptualization of service quality, one that accounts for the fundamentally human process of producing and delivering the product.

Jan Carlzon, president of Scandinavian Airlines System, deserves credit for adapting the metaphor "the moment of truth" from the lexicon of bullfighting. Carlzon told his people, "We have 50,000 moments of truth each day in our business." In Carlzon's conception of service, the company exists in the minds of its customers only during those incidents when they come into direct contact with specific aspects of its operation.

"If you think about it for a moment," he says, "you quickly realize that SAS, or any other airline, *is* the contact between one customer in the market and one SAS employee working at the front line. And when this contact appears, then SAS exists. These are the moments of truth, in which we show whether we are a good airline or a bad airline."

In service management terminology, a moment of truth—or M.O.T.—is:

The moment of truth: any episode in which the customer comes into contact with any aspect of the organization and gets an impression of the quality of its service.

The service management point of view suggests that these many moments of truth are the basic building blocks of the service product. The moment of truth is the basic atom of service, the smallest indivisible unit of value delivered to the customer. In my formulation of the service management model, I have taken Carlzon's metaphor of the moments of truth quite literally and have used it as a way to concretize the conception of service as a product.

What is the service you produce and deliver? The moments of truth—no more, no less. Physical products may be part of the interaction with the customer at the moments of truth, but the moments of truth themselves are really the product.

If you take the moments-of-truth concept literally and con- cretely, you forget about jobs and tasks and organizational struc- tures and procedures, and you start thinking in terms of *outcomes*. You can immediately begin to take an inventory of the moments of truth your customers experience as your frontline people deliver the service. Once you know what these moments of truth are, you can analyze every one of them from the standpoint of quality. You can start improving those that need improving and looking for ways to add value to all of them.

Some typical moments of truth, say in an air-travel experi- ence, are:

1. Customer calls the airline for information.
2. Customer books the flight with the airline representative.
3. Customer arrives at airport counter.
4. Customer waits in line.
5. Ticket agent invites customer to the counter.
6. Ticket agent processes payment and issues ticket.
7. Customer goes looking for the departure gate.
8. Gate agent welcomes customer to the flight, validates boarding pass.

9. Customer waits in departure lounge for flight to depart.
10. Boarding agent takes customer's ticket and invites customer on board.
11. Customer boards airplane, is greeted by flight attendant.
12. Customer looks for his or her assigned seat.
13. Customer looks for a place to stow carry-on luggage.
14. Customer takes his or her seat.
15. Etc., etc.

You can continue the list to include all of the moments of truth the customer might experience in getting from one city to another. There can be many moments of truth, even if the flight is uneventful. If anything out of the ordinary happens, other moments of truth can occur.

A moment of truth is typically neither positive nor negative in and of itself. It is the outcome of the moment of truth that counts. Did the customer feel good about the price of the ticket? Did he or she find the right seat, or was the seat double-booked? Was the flight attendant friendly or surly? Did the flight leave on time, or was it delayed? If it was delayed, how caringly did the gate agent or pilot explain the delay to the passengers?

Keep in mind that not all moments of truth involve direct interaction between your employees and customers. When the customer sees an advertisement for your business, that's a moment of truth; it creates an impression. Driving by your facility is, for the customer, a moment of truth. Entering a parking lot, walking into a lobby and getting an impression of the place, receiving a bill or a statement in the mail, listening to a recorded voice on the telephone, getting a package home and opening it, all of these are events that lead to an impression of your service. The sum total of all of the possible moments of truth your customers experience, both human and nonhuman, becomes your service image.

As you think about this new view of your product, in terms of moments of truth as episodes that offer perishable opportunities to make a quality impression, it becomes obvious that management is not in control of the quality. Managers can't be present at all of the moments of truth to supervise them and make sure employees handle them properly. This means they must rely on the working people who are handling the moments of truth. In fact, *they* are the managers at those moments; they are managing the moments of truth.

This is a provocative concept; every service employee is a manager, in a way. Each one controls the outcome of the moment of truth by having control over his or her own behavior toward the customer. If service people are apathetic, disagreeable, unfriendly, cold, distant, or uncooperative, their moments of truth go to hell in a handbasket. If they are lively, pleasant, warm, friendly, cooperative, and resourceful in taking care of the customer's problem, then their moments of truth shine, and the customer tends to generalize those experiences to your overall service image. It may be a frightening prospect for some managers: the ant army is in charge.

Sometimes this simple concept of moments of truth seems *too* simple for some managers. When I present it in seminars or in consultation situations, I occasionally find it necessary to repeat and reemphasize the definition of a moment of truth in order to help them think about it concretely. Sometimes they will nod their heads approvingly but will display no particular intellectual reaction. Later, when I test their understanding of the implications of the concept by asking them to itemize some moments of truth for their own organization, some of them draw a blank. The concept is elusively simple. Perhaps they have spent so many years thinking about tools and tasks that the shift to an outcomes orientation is confusing.

A typical seminar group of hotel managers, for example, when asked to form subgroups and produce newsprint posters listing all the moments of truth they could think of in their hotels, had trouble coming up with specific episodes. Some of them listed things like cleanliness, efficiency, and courtesy. In service management terms, those are *not* moments of truth. They may be important trait factors, but they are not *events*. A moment of truth is an *episode*—i.e., a specific event in time—in which the *customer* comes into *contact* with some aspect of the organization and gets an *impression* of its service.

The concept of moments of truth is one of the very basic foundation stones of the service management theory and will play a part in virtually all of the discussions of service quality to follow.

CRITICAL MOMENTS OF TRUTH

Not all moments of truth are created equal. A typical high-contact service business may have more than 100 different kinds of moments of truth, but usually only a few of them have a critical impact on the customers' perceptions.

Case in Point: A customer (patient) is lying in a hospital bed, having just been admitted to the hospital in preparation for tomorrow's surgery. A woman in a white uniform walks into the room carrying a tray that holds a hypodermic syringe and a few other implements. The customer looks up and realizes the syringe is meant for him. Put yourself in the customer's position for a few seconds. What would be going through your mind? Probably a number of questions, all of which relate to your personal sense of well-being.

You are asking yourself, "Who is this person? Is she someone in authority? Is she a nurse? Is she going to use that needle on me? Does she know what she's doing? How do I know she has the right room, the right person, and the right medication? Will this hurt? Why are they giving me an injection? What will it do to me? Are they going to explain anything to me, or just stick me with the needle?" For the customer, this is an important psychological event. It outranks many other moments of truth in its impact. It is not the same as the moment of truth of walking in the front door of the hospital, or going through the admitting procedures, or receiving a tray of food at the bedside. This one really *counts*. This is one of the *critical moments of truth* for the customer.

It may not seem very critical to the person administering the injection. Her system of priorities is much different from that of the customer. She may be thinking, "Nine more 'meds' to administer before I finish my shift. I'd better call Housekeeping to get that dirty-linen cart out of the hall. I wonder if Doctor X has calmed down and gotten over that mix-up on his patient's medication? Gee, I sure hope I can get a shot at that head nurse job. Gad, but my feet are tired. I'll be glad when this shift is over."

Here we have the basic ingredients of service success or service failure. If the service person is really thinking about service, she will focus her attention on the important elements of this moment of truth and handle it in such a way as to maximize the positive impact on the customer—or at least minimize the negative impact. What are some of the things she can do to handle this critical moment of truth effectively? She can:

1. Greet the customer cordially and reassuringly.
2. Introduce herself.
3. Give her undivided attention to the situation at hand.
4. Put the customer at ease with light conversation.
5. Explain the purpose and benefit of the medication.
6. Administer the injection in a gentle and caring way.
7. Make sure the customer is reasonably comfortable.
8. Inquire about any special needs or concerns.

On the other hand, if the service person is in a hurry, preoccupied, fatigued, bored, or simply insensitive, she may handle the whole moment of truth mechanically and impersonally, which is what happens much too often in health-care institutions. The combination of a critical moment of truth—i.e., one with significant impact for the customer—and an insensitive, uncaring, or incompetent service person is a prescription for disaster. The gap between the kind of treatment the customer was hoping for and what he actually experiences creates an especially negative feeling.

These critical moments of truth warrant special care and feeding. Managers can't be everywhere at once, so they need to choose carefully those aspects of the operation that have the highest potential impact—positive or negative—on the customer's satisfaction and repurchase intention. They need to keep these special aspects of the product under surveillance and help service people handle them effectively.

THE SERVICE TRIANGLE

One of the most basic elements of the service management model as presented in *Service America!*, and one that many managers quote to me in conversation, is the *service triangle*. It is worth repeating here for continuity, and it will play an important part in our analysis of the success factors involved in implementing a service initiative in almost any kind of organization.

I came upon the service triangle as a way of describing the operations of successful service businesses after looking at a great deal of research and commonsense knowledge about how the top service firms perform. Through all of my investigations, and in many discussions with executives of excellent (and mediocre) service companies, I discovered three major recurring characteristics that seemed to make all the difference. Virtually all of the excellent service businesses I know about have all three of these characteristics in good measure. Conversely, I can't think of a single service business that lacks any of these characteristics that ranks with the winners. These three key factors become the corners of the service triangle. They are:

1. A vision, or strategy for the service product.
2. Customer-oriented frontline people.
3. Customer-friendly systems.

The service triangle is a way of diagramming the interplay of these three critical elements, which must perform together to

FIGURE 2–1
The Service Triangle

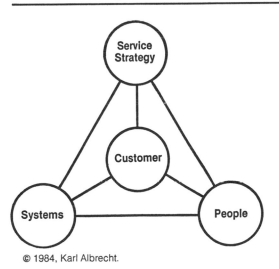

© 1984, Karl Albrecht.

maintain a high level of service quality. The following explanation comes verbatim from *Service America!*

> *A Well-Conceived Strategy for Service.* The outstanding organizations have discovered, invented, or evolved a unifying idea about what they do. This service concept, or service strategy as we shall call it in later discussions, directs the attention of the people in the organization toward the real priorities of the customer. This guiding concept finds its way into all that people do. It becomes a rallying cry, a kind of gospel, and the nucleus of the message to be transmitted to the customer.
>
> *Customer-Oriented Frontline People.* By some means the managers of such organizations have encouraged and helped the people who deliver the service to keep their attention fastened on the needs of the customer. The effective frontline person is able to maintain an "otherworldly" focus of attention by tuning in to the customer's current situation, frame of mind, and need. This leads to a level of responsiveness, attentiveness, and willingness to help that marks the service as superior in the customer's mind and makes him or her want to tell others about it and come back for more.
>
> *Customer-Friendly Systems.* The delivery system that backs up the service people is truly designed for the convenience of the customer rather than the convenience of the organization. The physical facilities, policies, procedures, methods, and communication processes all say to the customer, "This apparatus is here to meet your needs."

These three factors—a clear service strategy, customer-oriented frontline people, and customer-friendly systems—are all relatively simple in concept and fairly easy to understand. Yet making them a reality is almost always a monumental task, especially in large organizations. Most of the remainder of this book (*Service America!*) deals with what we have found out about implementing service management by trying to actively manage these three critical factors.

CYCLES OF SERVICE

I have often found it quite a task to get managers and frontline service people to switch their points of view and see their product as the customer sees it. Years of conditioning and familiarity with a service operation tend to distort one's perceptions. After you have administered thousands of injections, booked thousands of airline flights, sold thousands of plates of food or hotel rooms, or opened thousands of bank accounts, you may find it difficult to really appreciate the novice customer's point of view. He or she may be experiencing your process for the first time or on one of a few rare occasions. Understanding the reality of the customer's experience can be just as important as being an expert in your job tasks.

The technique I find most useful for helping people shift their points of view is to ask them to think about their product in terms of *cycles of service*. A cycle of service is the continuous chain of events the customer goes through as he or she experiences your service. This is the natural, unconscious pattern that exists in the customer's mind, and it may have nothing in common with your "technical" approach to setting up the business. You may be conditioned to think of your service operation in terms of the organizational departments and specialties that have to get involved in order to deliver the service.

But the customer seldom thinks in terms of departments or specialties. He or she usually thinks only in terms of having a need and having to take action to get that need met. The customer thinks in terms of an objective: I want a place to store my money; I want to eat a good meal in pleasant surroundings; I want to have my teeth cleaned; I want to see more clearly; I want to get to Buffalo in time for the wedding; I want to get my car working properly again.

It is common for service businesses to give their customers the runaround because of the way the businesses are organized. The customer turns the car over to the service-order writer, hoping to have it repaired. Returning to pick it up, he finds he must go to the cashier to get the keys and pay the bill. There is no one for him to talk to about the car—no one to answer his questions about the peculiar sound in the engine. If he doesn't like the bill or disagrees with the charge, the cashier may say, "I'm only the cashier. You'll have to see the service manager." When the customer asks, "Where is the service manager?" the answer might be, "He's gone for the day. You'll have to come back tomorrow." The customer may ask to speak to the mechanic who worked on the car, only to be told the mechanics aren't allowed to leave the shop to talk to customers.

Transfer this example to any other service industry or setting—banks, hotels, hospitals, financial services, food service, transportation (virtually all of the well-established business sectors)—and you can find variations on the same situation. If the customer has an unusual or complicated problem or a nonroutine need for which the business doesn't have a "system," it seems especially difficult for the organization to react to the customer in terms of his or her need rather than in terms of its internal structure. More repeat business has probably been driven away because people could not gain access to someone who could take care of their problem or alleviate their concerns than for any other reason.

The cycle-of-service concept helps people help the customer by getting them to reorganize their mental pictures of what goes on. Let's consider a typical cycle of service, such as getting a physical exam in a medical center. Here are some things you as a customer (patient) might go through:

1. Call the center for an appointment.
2. Drive to the center at the appointed time.
3. Find a parking place and park your car.
4. Enter the building and try to orient yourself.
5. Read the signs to find out where to go.
6. Ask for directions.
7. Take the elevator and walk through various corridors.
8. Check in at the administrative desk of the exam department.
9. Show your insurance card, fill out forms, etc.
10. Sit in the waiting area until your turn comes.
11. Go with the technical assistant into the exam area.
12. Have your vital signs taken (pulse, pressure, temperature).
13. Discuss your physical condition in an interview.
14. Go through a series of tests and measurements.
15. Have an exit interview with a medical person.
16. Check out and pay your bill.
17. Find your way out of the center and back to your car.
18. Drive out of the parking lot.
19. Wait for the results of your exam.

20. Receive the results, read, and react to them.
21. Call the center for follow-up treatment if necessary.

Figure 2–2 illustrates the cycle of service.

Notice that each of the items listed above is a *moment of truth* for you as a customer. Each is an episode in which you come into contact with some aspect of the organization and get an impression of the quality of its service. The various moments of truth form a continuous *chain of events* for you, the customer. Even though you may deal with 10 or 15 separate organizational departments, it is all one process to you.

Yet the providers of the service typically don't think of the process as a single flow of connected experiences. They think of it in terms of their own individual tasks and responsibilities. The admitting department thinks of you in terms of insurance coverage, personal statistics, and forms to be filled in. The technical assistant thinks of you as one of a number of people who form a line of traffic, which must be kept moving. The blood drawers, electrocardiogram specialists, X-ray technicians, and all the other pokers and thumpers who conduct the individual tests and measurements

FIGURE 2–2
The Cycle of Service

The Cycle of Service

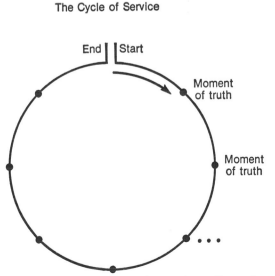

The cycle of service shows the service as the customer experiences it.

think of you as a source of blood to be analyzed, a beating heart to be measured, or a thorax to be X-rayed. The physician, nurse practitioner, or whoever conducts the personal interview sees you as an entity to be screened statistically. You either have something that needs treatment or you don't. If you don't, you fall into one category. If you do, he or she needs to follow up with a referral to a specialty department.

This is not to say there is anything wrong with any of the perceptions just enumerated. The world is full of specialists, and they have to be organized somehow. But at the same time, we must recognize that:

> **Sometimes the customer is the only one who sees the big picture.**

This is a very important fact, especially with large and complex service businesses. Each specialist has his or her arms around one leg of the elephant; only the customer sees the whole elephant. And some parts of the elephant—or the cycle of service—are left largely to chance. Review the list of moments of truth in the example above and see how many of them are "miscellaneous" in their impact on the customer. Parking the car, entering the building, finding the department, waiting, and moving from place to place are all moments of truth for the customer, but typically no one has any specific responsibility for the customer's well-being at those points. When he or she shows up on the horizon of another department, that group of specialists takes the ball.

Just like the moment-of-truth concept, the cycle of service is a powerful idea for helping service people shift their points of view and see things as the customers see them. Analyzing and improving cycles of service is a basic part of the "engineering" process of service management.

SPECIAL PROBLEMS OF SMALL
SERVICE BUSINESSES

Although service management has a strong appeal for medium- and large-sized organizations, many smaller service businesses can use it effectively as well. A smaller operator has certain issues and problems the mega-operation doesn't have, but may also have certain advantages. Indeed, some would contend a large service business should operate as much as possible like a collection of small businesses, with each keeping as close and responsive to the customer as possible.

Remember that bigger is not always better; consider the dinosaur. According to some theorists, the dinosaur was so big and its nervous system was so slow that if something hit it on the tail, it would take several seconds for the signal to get to its brain. This is the way many large organizations seem to operate. In a sense, the dinosaurs represent the Chapter 11 of evolutionary history. Being light on your feet can represent a significant competitive advantage if you're going up against the big companies.

It is worth exploring here some key aspects of this small service operation.

Some disadvantages of being a small operation compared to a large one can be:

You usually don't have the benefit of image or name recognition.

Luxury-level quality may require capital investment beyond your means.

You often don't have price efficiency working for you.

Your mistakes are usually more costly; small size is unforgiving.

It may be more difficult to attract qualified people.

On the other hand, some advantages of a smaller service business can be:

There is less organizational inertia, i.e., rules and customs.

You can change the organization more easily.

You can change or reposition the product more easily.

You can make your values as a leader more tangibly felt.

Leadership is closer to the working people.

It's easier to maintain team spirit and a sense of common purpose.

You can develop people on a more personal basis.

Another positive aspect of small service business is that you can usually try something new more quickly and find out whether it works. Many of the real innovations in service start in the hands of small companies. A typical small-business service, for example, is the concierge type of operation, which runs errands of every conceivable nature for busy executives. This type of low-capital business is ideal for the small operator, whereas it wouldn't be attractive to the large firm that must turn over a high gross revenue to stay in business.

In a smaller business, you may be able to achieve a level of service quality that outshines that of your larger competitors and thus capture a piece of the market and hold on to it. It is generally much more difficult for a huge organization to lift its game and move from so-so quality to outstanding quality, whereas it may be fairly easy for the small, highly adaptable company. Your problem is more like teaching a small dog to dance compared to their problem of teaching an elephant to dance.

HOW THE CHAMPIONS DO IT

If you contrast the ways of doing business exhibited by Level 5 organizations—those whose service quality is legendary—with those at levels 1, 2, or 3, you can discover certain characteristic and very important differences. Just as a champion athlete has patterns and habits that place him or her in a different league from the rest of us, so too the service champions have certain special qualities that make them champions. I've spent a great deal of time trying to isolate these winning characteristics. Here are some of the key ones I have identified so far.

They have the basics down pat. They realize that a quality product, delivered for a fair price and produced at an acceptable cost, is the starting point for service success. They grasp the fact that no amount of extras, special touches, or fancy packaging will overcome the limitations of a mediocre product. They start with the basics and never let their attention wander from the basics. They build service excellence upon a strong foundation of customer approval of the primary quality of the service they deliver. J. Willard Marriott, Sr., the late founder of the Marriott Corporation, was tireless and virtually obsessed in his attention to the details of quality. He would walk into any hotel kitchen or catering department and talk with the people about getting things right. Leon Leonwood Bean, founder of the highly respected L. L. Bean direct-mail company that ships millions of dollars in sporting goods and personal effects from a small town in Maine, said, "Sell good merchandise at a reasonable profit, treat your customers like human beings, and they'll always come back for more."

They believe quality drives profit.   The top leaders of the excellent service companies start with *quality,* not cost, in evaluating the effectiveness of their operations. They believe that if the quality is there in good measure, the profits will be there too when it's time to balance the books. In contrast, the leaders of mediocre service businesses tend to be compulsively and fearfully preoccupied with costs and profits, hoping that somehow the quality will take care of itself. This is a very difficult point for many executives in mediocre service firms to grasp. It also eludes many middle managers, even if their executives firmly believe in it. Years of conditioning and pressure from senior management teaches frontline people in these firms—and especially their supervisors—to be money oriented rather than quality oriented in their thinking. The entire reward system of the organization tends to orbit around this one key message: keep your costs in line. This difference in attitude is fundamental to the very psyche of the organization. John Kapioltas, chairman of the Sheraton Corporation, says, "Sheraton is a bottom-line, profit-oriented company. We believe the engine which drives those profits is personal, quality service."

They know their customers.   They are virtually obsessed with understanding the customer interface of the organization and making sure they are in tune with the customer's needs, attitudes, perceptions, values, and buying motivations. They continually conduct research into customer perceptions, and they make sure their key people understand the implications of the research. They start and end with the perceptions of their customers in defining the service product and in keeping it up to date. To these service champions, the customer is all—the alpha and the omega, the beginning and the end. Jim Nordstrom, president of the small Nordstrom chain of high-service department stores, says, "We encourage all of our sales people to form personal, long-term relationships with their customers and to get to know their needs and wants. It's not uncommon for one of them to call a customer and let him or her know about a sale that's coming up, or a special item of merchandise that we've acquired. They have a sixth sense about their customers."

They have a "moments of truth" focus in their operations. They think in terms of customer impact rather than in terms of jobs, tasks, rules, departments, and procedures. This factor also involves a profound shift in point of view, which I will discuss more fully later. The service champions tend to be *outcome oriented* rather than tool-and-task oriented. They start with a different "feel" for what the business is all about. They do not allow themselves to become so introverted in their day-to-day operations that they lose their customer focus. Jan Carlzon, president of Scandinavian Airlines, says, "The only thing that counts in the new SAS is a satisfied customer. We are not brokers and custodians of fixed assets like aircraft. We can have as many aircraft as we want, but if people don't want to fly with us, it's worth nothing. Service is what counts."

They have a "whatever it takes" attitude. They focus on solving the customer's problem and meeting the customer's need, not on just doing the day's work. They are willing to do the unusual when it's warranted. They are willing to bend the rules occasionally and to give in to the customer from time to time when it's appropriate to the situation. They look upon an unusual request from the customer as an opportunity to add value to their service product, not as a disturbance to their daily routines. They are willing to go the extra mile for the customer, knowing that an occasional small investment of time and cost can pay big dividends in the long run. Dick Scott, chief operating officer of Longs Drug Stores, brags about an assistant store manager who picked up a customer's photographs from the processing lab and dashed to the airport to give them to her minutes before she boarded a plane to return to Poland. The pictures were priceless memories of her visit with her relatives in California. Her father, living in California, wrote Scott a touching letter in his limited English to say how grateful he was for the store manager's thoughtfulness. According to Scott, "By any financial measure you can apply, we lost money on that sale; in fact, we lost our fanny. Or did we?"

They recover skillfully from the inevitable blunders. They maintain a collective sense of responsibility that crosses organizational boundaries. In the excellent service businesses, each person feels responsible to contribute to the customer outcome. They do not brush the customer off or give him or her the runaround, and when something goes wrong they fix it, instead of pointing fingers at one another. They know there will be the inevitable mistakes, slipups, and downright screwups. They recognize that successful recovery from a malfunction can have a huge impact on the customer's perception and on word-of-mouth referral.

Service happens inside the company as well as outside. Internal departments who may never see customers accept their responsibilities to contribute to the ultimate moments of truth that make the product. They focus on making an important contribution to the total process of serving the customer. According to Stephen Sweeney, chairman of the Boston Edison Company, "Very few of our employees, perhaps 10 percent or less, actually deal directly with the customer; we are largely an 'invisible' service company. But we believe in a *total service concept,* which means that everybody in the company has to work together as a service team, each department helping the other, so the total product meets the customer's needs."

They see management as a helper and supporter. Jan Carlzon, president of Scandinavian Airlines, told his managers, "You are not here to dictate to the front line. You are here to help them, to support them. And when they ask you for help, you have to listen to them, and not the other way around." Over and above the responsibility to set direction, establish priorities, and make decisions, managers in the outstanding service companies see themselves as charged with the mission of enabling the frontline people to serve their customers effectively. They ask, "What can we in management do to help you get your jobs done?"

They care about their employees as well as their customers. J. Willard (Bill) Marriott, Jr., the second-generation leader of the $5 billion Marriott Corporation, speaks to managers in his company on a regular basis. He always says the same thing, "Take care of your employees and they'll take care of your customers." This does not necessarily mean higher pay than the rest of the industry, or lavishly expensive benefit programs, or other forms of material payoffs. But it does mean attentive, caring leadership, which treats the employee like a somebody rather than like a number or an interchangeable part in a production process. The top service companies tend to have staff-relations policies that mirror their customer-relations policies.

They are perpetually unsatisfied with their performance. They are constantly looking for ways to improve or refine their service product. They measure and evaluate their quality on an ongoing basis and look for areas that may need attention. However effective they might be, they are never willing to accept the status quo. David Ogilvy, head of the huge Ogilvy & Mather advertising firm in New York, gave an example of this kind of corporate attitude about the product. His firm had developed an ad campaign for Rolls-Royce, emphasizing the quality of the product. His proposed ad showed a person cruising along in a Rolls, with a title under the photo that declared: "At 55 miles per hour, the loudest sound you can hear in a Rolls-Royce is the ticking of the clock." As he went into a meeting to discuss the ad concept with the company's executives, the chief engineer tossed the ad slicks on the conference table and said with disgust, "We've got to do something about that damned clock."

CHAPTER 3

OFF TO A FLYING STOP?

Enthusiasm, n. A distemper of youth, curable by small doses
of repentance in connection with outward applications of experience.

> —*Ambrose Bierce*
> *The Devil's Dictionary*

GREAT EXPECTATIONS

There is nothing quite like the excitement of a new idea, especially
one that holds the promise of making a big difference in the business fortunes of a company. Time and again I have had the pleasure
of seeing executives and managers light up over the prospects of
adopting service quality as a competitive weapon. And the service
management model has a way of seizing their attention and truly
inflaming their imaginations.

They talk enthusiastically, glowingly, and aggressively about
making service the primary driving idea for the business. They
fantasize about how great it's going to be when all of the frontline
people are performing at their peak and managing the moments of
truth creatively and effectively.

They have a gleam in their collective eye when they talk about
tracking down and eliminating the organizational sacred cows that
interfere with people's ability to give outstanding service. They're
ready to clean house.

One of the things executives often say when they are in this
altered state of consciousness is something on the order of, "This
is the first time we've really had a focus for our business. This is
something we can all get behind and work to make happen. Finally, we can go to the employees with a direction that makes

sense. It's something everybody in the organization can get excited about."

It's always a delight for me to see this energy and enthusiasm. It's almost as if they have discovered the fountain of youth or something equally valuable. And it's with a touch of sympathy that I watch them reenter the world of reality, as they begin to realize over the next some months that believing it doesn't automatically make it happen. Gradually, the awful truth sets in: it will take a great deal of time, energy, money, patience, and dogged persistence to raise the quality of service to an outstanding level.

As Mark Twain observed about his experiences in traveling to California to get rich in the gold rush: "I struck a great disappointment when I discovered you had to dig for the gold with a long-handled shovel. I thought all you had to do was scoop it up off the ground."

THE SEARCH FOR A QUICK FIX

It is probably a combination of this early rush of excitement and the natural bias toward decisive action that most executives have that makes them vulnerable to the appeal of quick-fix approaches to service. They want action, and they want it now. In the words of the fictitious chief executive who just discovered the idea of corporate culture, "That sounds great! I want one by Monday morning."

Executives who are very experienced, well educated, and sophisticated about their markets and their products are often remarkably naive about organizational culture and process. Many of them, often without realizing it, want to handle the people and processes of the organization with the same mechanistic approaches they use in dealing with product design, acquisition of capital equipment, or project management. People are more difficult to deal with than things, so it becomes very tempting to deal with them as if they were things.

Many of the social-cultural mistakes executives make in launching new programs, such as service quality programs, originate in this nonhuman, mechanistic world view, as well as in a certain naivete about how people in large numbers respond to authority and direction. This style of operating seems to be "ready, fire, aim." It's over before it starts.

For example, it is not uncommon to see executives of large companies simply declare, by executive fiat, that there will be excellent service to the customer. They will make a few pronouncements at the board meeting, or the executive staff meeting, or the operations management meeting and assume their wishes will somehow magically become the guiding spirit for everyone at the working level.

They may issue policies and directives—another mechanistic attempt at inducing action. They may make inspiring statements in the company newsletter—or even worse, in the public press—about how service oriented the company is. They may create special executive positions or departments charged with customer service.

And, of course, there is the ever-popular annual management meeting. This is the gathering of the clan, often at a resort location, where senior management communicates progress and direction to the managers of the organization. There may be motivational video programs, slide shows, specially written sound tracks with rock and march music. The quick-fix approach is to bring in a speaker at one of these meetings, to get everybody excited about service.

The wave of interest in service management has broadened the market for motivational speakers. More and more of them are putting themes like "customer service," "get close to your customer," and "the customer comes first" into their material. This is not to say motivational speeches do no good, but I believe they have little lasting effect unless they fit into the context of an overall organizational approach to service excellence.

The problem with most quick-fix approaches is that they are top heavy. That is, they start at the top of the organization and they usually don't go much further. There is little in the way of concrete action and follow-through to the grass-roots level of everyday work.

A remarkable number of executives seem to believe that all they have to do is tell their direct-report managers what they want, and their desires will somehow percolate down through the levels of the organization to be fully understood and acted upon by the frontline staff. The reality is that the sense of clarity, excitement, urgency, and determination gets diminished by about 50 percent every time it makes the transition from one layer of the bureaucracy to the next lower layer. The chief may be tremendously excited about the new direction, but those who report to him or her come away from the meeting about half as excited. They communicate it to their subordinates, who come away half as excited as they are, and so on it goes, down through the monkey bars until it reaches the lowest level employee—if it ever does.

It's a strange feeling for an executive to realize that, regardless of the amount of formal authority he or she has, even a simple directive doesn't trickle down through the organization undistorted or undiminished. The more complex, abstract, or conceptual messages often don't trickle down at all. He or she may be in charge, but can really influence the masses only to the extent that the message has concrete significance and personal impact. Most executives realize at some point in their careers that you can't legislate feelings, values, and commitment.

One of Napoleon's most revealing comments, made at the height of his power and influence as leader of the *Grande Armee,* was, "Do you know what amuses me the most? The utter impotence of force to *organize* anything."

What we have learned about organizational life is that, if executives want to mobilize the people of the organization to a new philosophy of excellence, they must find a way to make that direction meaningful and exciting to the people and communicate it to them in such a way that they fully grasp, at a personal level, the value of embracing it. This is almost always a tall order.

Those executives who are realistic about what it takes to achieve excellence in service understand that they have to start with a sense of determination coupled with stubbornly high expectations of themselves, their managers, and their organization. And they have to be willing to "keep on keeping on" until they get where they need to be.

We have to be willing to recognize that, in some cases—perhaps most—the elephant doesn't particularly want to dance. Frequently, there are factors built into the organization or its social culture that present an inertial resistance to the efforts of top management to mobilize the troops for the mission of service.

This is not to say that working people don't want to do a good job, or that they would be unwilling to put forth an outstanding effort on behalf of the customer. Indeed, we know that the vast majority of working people crave meaning and satisfaction from their work, and that relatively few of them get it. Most of them are hungry for the chance to do something for a living that they can be proud of, and they can invest remarkable levels of energy in their moments of truth if they feel that way about their jobs.

As we have known for centuries, mobilizing people to constructive action is less a matter of motivating them than it is of getting rid of the factors that *demotivate* them. So, if we're going to make service excellence the strategic focus of a business, we have to go to work on the organization itself. We have to find and eliminate the demotivators, the disincentives, and the obstacles to belief. We first have to create the conditions that enable the elephant to want to dance. Then we can get on with the job of teaching.

CHAPTER 4

COMMON BLUNDERS IN LAUNCHING SERVICE PROGRAMS

We have met the enemy, and they is us.
—*Pogo (cartoon character)*

Sometimes we can be our own worst enemies when it comes to instituting significant changes in the corporate culture. Executives who should know better can be amazingly naive and shortsighted when they get fired up with the desire to make wall-to-wall organizational changes. In their optimistic zeal and missionary fervor, they can easily lose sight of some of the most basic realities of organizational life. They can do some of the most self-defeating things in their naive belief that might makes right, and vice versa.

In organizations that have tried unsuccessfully to launch service-quality initiatives, the programs often went off the track because they were not properly thought through at the outset. So many of these organizations, lacking a common vision and philosophy about quality and lacking the internal expertise to implement change-management interventions, end up with ill-conceived campaigns that fizzle out.

There are lots of ways to shoot yourself in the foot when you try to take a total service campaign out into an organization. In fact, there are probably more ways to do it wrong than there are ways to do it right. While observing and working with companies that have tried to launch service initiatives, I have seen certain kinds of blunders committed over and over again. It seems only fair to catalog these most common blunders, so some people may spare themselves the frustration and disappointment of going down those dead-end roads. After all, why repeat the mistakes of others just for the sake of learning by experience? Why not learn from others, and at least make some original blunders of your own?

In this chapter, I identify and analyze the most common mistakes executives tend to make in launching service quality programs in their organizations, and I offer suggestions about how to avoid them. The mistakes discussed in the following pages are not the only ones by any means, but they are some of the most common and most preventable.

MISREADING THE CUSTOMER

Perhaps the cardinal rule of service management is:

Know thy customer.

I've just about concluded that, the longer you're in a particular business, the higher the odds you don't really understand your customer. It's easy to ride along on intuitive guesswork over the years, assuming you know what your customers will and won't buy. It's also easy to get surprised—either by your competitors or by your customer.

Ego factors operating in the minds of executives and middle managers may make it difficult for them to accept the idea of investigating the perceptions of their customers about the product. Old-timers who have been in the industry since it began may say, "I know what our customers want. I don't need any fancy market research people with Ph.D.s and computers to tell me what I already know." Others may pride themselves on the service their companies provide and may resent the implication that there could be any shortfall in quality.

Ego is probably the biggest obstacle to learning and adaptation. If you don't believe you have anything to learn, and if you conceive of the process of investigating and learning as giving evidence that you don't really know your business, then you are likely to block your own adaptation.

A number of times over the past four years or so that I've been working with the service management model I've been surprised to discover that assumptions I'd held about certain service businesses didn't hold true. I've also been surprised at how often the assumptions of the experts—i.e., the executives of companies in that industry—didn't hold water.

Customer perception research, which we will discuss in depth in a later chapter, can shed light on previously undiscovered aspects of the customer's needs and motivations. The top service companies are virtually always investigating various aspects of the customer interface and exploring new possibilities for offering value.

One of my favorite stories illustrates the impact of not knowing what your customers want. An elderly couple went into a doctor's office, asking to be examined together. When their turn came, the receptionist escorted them into the examining room to see the doctor.

"What can I do for you?" inquired the doctor. "Well," replied the elderly gentleman, "we would like to have you observe us while we make love." The doctor was a bit taken aback, but acceded to the request. Afterward, the senior citizens got dressed, paid the fee, and left without further comment. The doctor was rather amazed and a bit confused, but chalked it up as one of those strange things that happen in the course of a medical career.

Two weeks later, the episode was repeated. "We would like you to observe while we make love," instructed the gentleman. After a similar episode, the couple again paid the fee and left.

When they showed up for the third time a few weeks later, the doctor simply couldn't go on with the process. "Listen, folks," he said. "I suppose it's none of my business, but you've got to admit this is a strange request. You haven't asked me for an examination, or a medical opinion, or anything. What's going on here?"

"Oh, it's simple," replied the gentleman. "You see, we're not married to each other—we're having an affair. The Holiday Inn charges $60 a night; you charge $40, and we get $25 back from Medicare. So you're our best deal."

Sometimes the customer's behavior makes sense only when you really understand what he or she is trying to buy.

LACK OF A CLEAR BUSINESS FOCUS

Many executives would like to have excellent service without having to get into the service business. They want to get ahead of their competitors, enjoy the respect and loyalty of their customers, and have the economic benefits of an excellent service image. They just don't want to have to get involved.

There is a very strong temptation to conceive of service as some vague, nebulous feeling in the company—especially among the frontline workers. Service is caring. Service is putting the customer first. Service is all of the frontline people being nice to the customer. The workers should be excited about service; they should want to give excellent service to all customers; they should be proud of the company and proud to work there. The only problem with wanting people to feel this way is that they usually *don't* feel this way without having good reasons.

So many discussions about service quality that go on in corporate conference rooms are merely an exchange of platitudes. Without a clear focus—a driving idea, together with a clear direction for implementing the idea—the discussions never get out of the warm fuzzy stage. Focus is necessary to transform these great ideas into crude deeds.

Without a business focus, and a way of converting that focus into concrete action at the front line, any organization whose leaders are interested in service quality will simply drift about hoping for a miracle. The employees will hear the talk, and some will respond in their own best ways, but if no one comes to them with concrete approaches and expectations, they will continue on much as before.

Setting forth a strong, unambiguous focus for the organization is one of the most difficult and challenging things top management can do. To say to people, "We have one single priority in this organization—one primary driving idea," is a very bold thing for a top manager to do. Most do not have the fortitude to live with the consequences of such a clear statement of organizational direction. It is one thing to talk glowingly about the importance of customer service, but it is another matter to get personally involved in implementing it on a day-to-day basis. One can see the impact and value of a clear service focus at the basic, grass-roots level of the everyday work. It keeps people awake and energized. It keeps managers on their toes. And it keeps a large number of people on the same wavelength for a substantial period of time.

MIXED MESSAGES TO THE EMPLOYEES

Think about what a typical working person in a large organization sees and hears during a typical workday—from the boss, from peers, and from the grapevine. There are messages passing back and forth all day long, and many of them are silent, implicative, unspoken meanings. Anything top management wants the worker to hear, know, and believe must compete with and become more valid than this day-to-day stream of consciousness.

It is amazingly easy to be misunderstood when you are the chief executive and you send out the word about some new undertaking. However simple, clear, and valid the idea may seem to you, it is easily twisted, distorted, contaminated with unintended interpretations, and simply misheard. As if this naturally occurring handicap in organizational communications were not enough to contend with, some executives succeed in further confusing the situation by trying to say more than one thing at the same time.

One of the most popular ways to confuse and unsettle employees, and especially junior managers, is for top management to talk about service quality and doing right by the customer one day and cost reduction and cost control the next. This gives rise to the "but" syndrome: we want excellent service, *but* keep your costs in line. Think service, *but* reduce staff and cut your budget. It is possible to pursue resource reduction efforts in conjunction with service improvement efforts, but it is necessary to communicate the rationale for the efforts very carefully, skillfully, and clearly.

The mixed-message syndrome often occurs because top management is unable or unwilling to prioritize in a global way. All too often executives cannot bring themselves to point the direction clearly and simply and stick to it. Sometimes it is a simple lack of executive leadership, and sometimes it is a matter of personality or the individual executive's intellectual orientation. Some executives believe things like mission statements, strategy statements, and clearly stated priorities are simply impediments to their freedom to manage. They want to meet each day anew, with a new approach to the problems of the day, unfettered by the commitments of yesterday. Unfortunately, this usually keeps their direct-report managers baffled and makes it very difficult for those managers to communicate any sense of direction or focus to frontline employees.

When there are mixed messages, employees tend to choose the messages they want to hear and respond to. They can't accept or believe in any one clear focus, because the focus always seems to be changing. In this kind of situation, it is very difficult to get a service program rolling with any kind of enthusiasm or support from lower-level managers or staff people.

BRASS BANDS, ARM BANDS, AND LAPEL BUTTONS

Many executives really believe that an internal motivation campaign is all it takes to make great service happen. They seem to think the employees are rather simpleminded, naive creatures who just need a pep talk every now and then.

The methods are fairly standard: hold pep rallies for all employees; put up posters with nifty slogans about how The Customer Is King; and issue arm bands, T-shirts, lapel buttons, and cash-register stickers that will remind everyone every day to do a good job for the customer. Show them motivational video tapes starring the president of the company exhorting them to do better. Write jingles and set them to music.

Usually the junior managers get a taste of the same motivational fudge. Most large organizations will have annual management meetings where top management can explain progress and direction to everyone on the management team. Sometimes these meetings become kickoff sessions for the new motivational campaign. Multimedia shows portray the excitement of the new campaign. Fifteen-projector slide shows set to rock music, beautifully produced video shows, and motivational speakers lend an emotional intensity to the event.

But without effective follow-through, these kinds of entertainment-oriented motivational campaigns usually fizzle. That's all the employees take them for—entertainment. They're fun while they last, but they don't have any connection to the day-to-day work.

Drama, entertainment, and motivational efforts can play an important part in gaining commitment for a service initiative, but only when they are used properly and at the right times. When the culture and climate are right, and when the organization is fully committed to a clear direction and a concrete program, it is often appropriate and effective to dramatize the effort with various energy-raising techniques. But it is critically important that the high-energy methods support an overall implementation process and not stand alone as the only evidence of management commitment.

SMILE TRAINING

Smile training is another popular fix with executives who want to do something quick and noticeable. I use the term *smile training* to denote the style and intent of such training, not to disparage the general idea of training frontline people in service skills. Effective training almost always has a useful place in a major service initiative, but the key word is *effective*. I call it smile training when it:

Is so absurdly simple that it insults the intelligence of the employees.

Condescends to them or treats them like children.

Assumes or implies they are inept or ineffective in their jobs.

Purports to teach them trivial things, e.g., literally how to smile at the customer.

Some human resource development specialists refer to this kind of mass smile training as the "spray and pray" approach. You round them up and give them all a shot from a figurative spray can, hoping they will all be transformed. Others, especially employees, refer to it as "charm school." I sometimes refer to it as hosing them down and delousing them—figuratively, of course.

The difference between smile training and effective training is basically in the intent and approach. If the approach is to blame customer satisfaction problems on the frontline people, and assume they somehow have to be fixed, they're basically guilty until proven innocent. If the intent is to run them all through a kind of mass educational car wash and assume they will be better people, then I call it smile training. Training is potentially effective if it:

Helps the employees understand their customers better.

Treats them like mature people.

Is relevant to their own jobs and lives.

Addresses their specific needs and concerns.

Includes useful personal skills that can help them deal with the stresses of contact jobs.

Fits into an overall program of service quality.

Is followed up by reinforcement and support back on the job.

SHORT ATTENTION SPAN (OR, "THIS MONTH'S THEME IS . . .")

One of the best ways for executives to lose credibility with the frontline employees, as well as their subordinate managers, is to jump from one fad idea to another without following through on any of them. Some executives are particularly susceptible to "the latest thing." One month it's zero-based budgeting. The next month it's communication training. Then it's management by objectives. Next it's one-minute management. Some go for sensitivity training, est, and other variations on personal growth. Quality circles look good—let's try that. And now it's time for customer service. This is the "theme of the month" approach.

The problem with this short-attention-span syndrome is that nothing lasts long enough to show results. Just as the noise and hoopla are at their peak, the boss discovers some new latest thing and runs off in that direction. After a few cycles of flirtation with new fads, the employees know that none of them will last. So they just shrug their shoulders every time a new one comes along and assume it will be no different from the last. When executives operate this way for any length of time, the employees begin to conclude that they don't really know what they are doing. They can't detect a common direction, a single driving priority, or a meaningful message from senior management. They have no choice but to conclude there isn't one.

It makes more sense to choose one theme or focus, regardless of what it is, and exploit it in depth rather than switch from one to another. The payoff in reduced confusion and lost energy alone will be worth it, even if the theme is not a very good one. If it is good, so much the better.

ONE MORE PROGRAM (OR, "THIS TIME IT'S FOR REAL")

Some organizations have a history of piling one new "program" on top of another. Each one deals with a grave, new pressing issue. There is a big sales drive. Next there's a merchandising drive for certain products. Then comes the cost reduction program. Next we need a productivity improvement program. That's followed by a loss control program. Now it's a paperwork reduction program. Then comes quality control, and on and on it goes.

When the time comes to launch a really significant program, top management has cried wolf so many times that the people can't tell the biggie from all the rest.

Sometimes it gets to the point that the chief executive or another of the senior executives will decide that there is no such thing as a "program" any more. They realize that the people in the organization, especially the middle managers, have been so overprogrammed that it becomes necessary to trick them into seeing the new one as unique and special. "This is not a 'program,' " they intone solemnly. "This goes far beyond any program we have ever done before. This is a new way of life." The employees and most of their managers just yawn and go back to work.

When everything is a priority, nothing is really a priority. People can get excited just so many times. After that, they wear out. One of the reasons for this program overload can be a perpetual emergency syndrome on the part of senior management. Everything has to happen *now*. There is never enough time to think something through and do it effectively. Lack of planning, lack of preparation, and lack of advance notice down through the ranks means each new big program will catch people off guard again. They don't see it coming, and they don't have time to get comfortable with the idea before it hits them. This leads to constant upheaval as the managers try to fit one program after another into the day's work.

Program overload can also result from a lack of delegation of responsibility, authority, and entitlement to think to the lower levels of the organization. When top management holds the reins too tightly, keeps the critical information to itself, and refuses to give middle and junior managers freedom to act, the organization tends to freeze up. With nothing new or innovative happening at the lower levels, top management feels it has to be the inventor of every new initiative. Executives don't realize that lack of energy and initiative throughout the organization is a problem of their own making. By loosening the reins a bit and encouraging junior managers to think and act on their own initiative, they can eliminate the need for so many top-down programs.

RIGOR MORTIS

In some organizations there has to be a policy, a program, a procedure manual, or a rule book for just about anything. This is a typically American syndrome stemming from the manufacturing mentality, and it becomes a religion in highly structured organizations operating in mature industries that change relatively little over time.

A characteristic approach to service improvement in these organizations is to rewrite all the job descriptions so they will include service standards. These standards may be meaningless or irrelevant to the customer's needs, but the managers get a warm feeling knowing they exist.

One organization I worked with, a company that operated 700 restaurants, approached the problem of service quality by creating a 150-item checklist for district managers to use in evaluating each restaurant. The program had virtually no provision for involvement of or contribution from frontline workers. It was a strictly normative, evaluative concept.

When this structured philosophy goes to its extreme, you have a fully developed rigor mortis situation. There will be a program director for the service program, with an office and appointed assistants. There will be interminable customer studies and analyses of jobs, systems, and departments. Managers will have to prepare and submit their service improvement plans. They will have to revise all job descriptions in their departments to include service standards. The program will create enough activity to give the impression that something is happening, but it is a clear case of paralysis by analysis.

It has been said that the last act of a dying organization is for somebody to put out a new policy manual. Rigor mortis organizations are so wedded to paper, policy, and procedure that this is their instinctive response in launching any new venture. They feel safe with rules and rituals. But this approach usually strangles the creativity and original thinking necessary to make bold new changes. Executives in these kinds of cultures need to learn to tolerate considerably more ambiguity in daily life and to be willing to authorize people at the lower levels to think.

FEATHER MERCHANTS

Some executives are suckers for every new management gimmick or slickly packaged new program that comes down the pike. Quite a few consultants and consulting firms specialize in organizational interventions of various kinds. Some of them are effective and some are not. Some of those who are not effective may nevertheless be very impressive to executives who have had little exposure to organizational development techniques. Many of them genuinely believe in their approaches. And some of them are just plain feather merchants—purveyors of consulting snake oil.

William Harrington, senior vice president of the Boston Edison Company, calls these kinds of consultants "fluff doctors." "They come in and make a lot of noise and use a lot of fancy language," he says. "But when you see what they're really doing, it doesn't amount to much."

Some feather merchants have a gift for making the most basic ideas seem suddenly new, esoteric, and exotic. They can take a simple principle of management, like planning, or goal setting, or employee communication, and dramatize it to the point where it takes on an almost overwhelming significance. They often employ a special lingo—a highly metaphorical or exotic terminology that makes their concepts and methods seem somehow larger than life.

These feather merchants may employ a special procedure or process, which they represent as their own mystical knowledge. They have some special know-how or expertise that they can put to use on behalf of the client organization, but that they somehow cannot teach to others.

They often enter the organization by selling one key executive on their personal chemistry and exotic techniques and having him or her act as their champion. Once in the organization, they try to create as much drama around themselves and their methods as possible and to make their influence as widely felt as possible, thereby justifying six-figure investments in their contracts.

Occasionally, an organization will have one or more organization development professionals on staff who are familiar with the various methods of cultural intervention. They can often sort out the feather merchants from those who offer promising models and methods. But usually, executives have no one to help them keep from falling in love with some approach because of its exotic nature. These executives are more likely to have their heads turned by aggressive and articulate feather merchants who are more style than substance.

GOON SQUADS

Goon squads, hit teams, swat teams—they go by various names— are shock troops sent in by management to "straighten out" service units that are in trouble. In some organizational cultures, if you don't perform, you get the ax. A prevailing "survival of the fittest" mentality accepts no excuses, tolerates no weakness, and allows no forgiveness. In this atmosphere, it may be customary for some in-house analysis group to "do a study" of the offending service unit or operation. The visit of the goon squad often gives rise to tremendous apprehension, anger, and animosity on the part of the people working in the target group. And justifiably so, because "being studied" is often the kiss of death for the manager of the unit in this kind of culture.

With the goon squad approach, it is not a cooperative, helpful intervention. It is a fault-finding mission from the start. This approach is most often used when there are profit problems, such as when the profit of a field operation falls below the cutoff level, but it can also be used when there are serious service problems. Sometimes the goon squad approach is used on whole companies, with the utility industry being a notorious example. Almost every public utility company in every state has been studied against its will at some time.

It is customary in the utility industry for a state regulatory body, i.e., the public utilities commission, to periodically declare that the gas and electric company is mismanaged and that it needs a good going-over by an outside consulting firm. This is often good box office for the commission, because it is, after all, a political body that wants the taxpayers to know it is defending their interests against the predations of this disreputable corporate goliath. So it is duly decreed that the utility company will hire a consulting firm and subject itself to a critical appraisal.

The consulting firm, which must be a large and well-known one, comes in and administers a ritual flogging to the company's management. The consultants conduct an exhaustive study, usually at a cost in the neighborhood of $1 million, of everything the company does. They look in all the file cabinets, interview hundreds of managers and workers, organize and analyze mountains of data, and finally submit their recommendations for improvement. Then the company executives are expected to accept all or most of the recommendations and implement them.

It all becomes a giant ritual of atonement. The company's management is accused from above, indicted by the consultant, found guilty, and convicted. The executives carry out the obligatory acts of contrition and finally receive forgiveness. A decade later it will probably happen again.

The same kind of thing can happen inside a service organization on a smaller scale when the culture is punitive rather than supportive. Top management perceives service problems as transgressions to be punished, rather than opportunities to improve, grow, and learn. Rather than make specialized consulting resources available to managers of units having problems, top management inflicts the consultants on the misbehaving units. This leads to animosity, resentment, and further erosion of loyalty and respect for executive leadership.

There is plenty of room for specialized assistance to service units, within the framework of cooperation, positive expectations, and shared responsibility for improvement. The managers and workers in the receiving unit or operation must see the assistance as for their benefit and aimed at helping them make the best possible contribution to company performance.

CHAPTER 5

COMMON PITFALLS IN
SERVICE PROGRAMS

> The only universal form of compulsory education is
> experience.
>
> *—Anonymous*

Over and above the most common mistakes executives can make in launching service-quality programs, there are a few typical ways in which they can get ambushed along the way. When service initiatives in organizations grind to a halt, it is typically because something about the situation in the organization itself is standing in the way. The right things don't happen if the right conditions are not in place. Here are some of the most common pitfalls that can derail a service program.

CULTURE AND CLIMATE PROBLEMS

A service initiative needs all the help it can get to take root and thrive in an organization. If we're going to get almost all of the people to raise their personal standards and their expectations of themselves and one another, the atmosphere has to be right. Certain key values have to be in place. There needs to be a fairly strong sense of optimism; people need to believe that such a thing is worthwhile and worth doing. There also has to be a reasonable level of teamwork and cooperation. And most of the people must have a reasonable sense of loyalty and identification with the organization in order for them to be willing to invest their energy and enthusiasm in a new venture.

It is my impression that a majority of business organizations have one or more significant aspects of their internal environment—their culture—out of whack with respect to what they need for service excellence. There may be turf problems in the form of conflicts, cross purposes, and feuds between departments or factions in the company. Lack of a common philosophy of vision can cause relationships among various sectors of the organization to degenerate to a "me-first" orientation. When people are feeling competitive or defensive, they are not likely to combine their ideas and energies in a joint effort aimed at a higher philosophical purpose.

There may be blocking factors within the culture itself. Certain norms, traditions, and rules for behavior may conspire to make people cautious, self-centered, and passive in their day-to-day activities. This tends to be especially true in large, highly structured organizations that operate in mature industries. Banks, for example, often have such confining rules and policies about risk and decision making that the people working there become robotically conditioned to do nothing when there is no rule to follow. Large insurance companies are often the same way. They are organized to minimize and control risk, and this risk-aversive philosophy tends to spread to all aspects of organizational life, well beyond the limits of financial risk.

Executive pressures may push people in unintended directions. As discussed in the previous chapter, the mixed messages employees get from the executive level can seem contradictory and self-canceling to them. The big, new motivational campaign can be saying, "Do everything you can to please the customer," while the older, more established, silent messages can be saying, "You'd better be keeping your costs down," or "Keep it moving; don't waste time with any one customer." The real message—the one that prevails in the long run—is the one that is hooked to the reward system. What you stroke is what you get.

The people in an organization might be in a very negative, pessimistic, or fearful frame of mind because of current circumstances. Health-care organizations in the United States, for example, have gone through very difficult times with declining business, cost reductions, and structural changes in the economics of the industry. When the employees in a hospital are facing the prospect of a layoff for the first time in the institution's history, people get fearful and disoriented. Professional nurses, for example, ask themselves, "Why should I stick around here and wait for the ax to fall on me? Why should I even stay in this profession when it's become so completely different from what it was when I started?"

When people are in pain, for whatever reasons, they find it difficult to get excited about anything, least of all about something as abstract and tenuous as "excellent service." The general atmosphere can work against executive attempts to show people that service quality might be a key to competitive survival. They become so preoccupied with their own survival that the idea of the organization's survival is too distant for them to deal with.

The rumor mill might also be contributing to a toxic cultural atmosphere. The organization's grapevine—the tribal drums that tell people what's *really* going on—may be carrying all sorts of pessimistic news, distorted predictions of dire fate, and outright untruths. But in a fear environment, people are likely to grasp at any piece of news, and they often seem to be more willing to embrace negative news than positive news.

This is why it becomes crucially important for executives to understand their organizational culture *before* trying to launch a service program. They need to know how ready the people are to undertake such a venture, and how they would be likely to react to it. If the soil is bitter, the tree is not likely to grow.

QUALITY OF WORK LIFE PROBLEMS

More and more organizations are using the concept of *quality of work life* as a single, unifying idea for understanding and managing culture. Quality of work life is the sum total of the individual working person's experiences with the company, as he or she perceives it. It is a personal, individual matter, not a cultural matter. If a person is well paid, has an enjoyable job, has a positive relationship with the boss, and sees opportunities to get ahead, then quality of work life is high for him or her. Conversely, if a person feels blocked, discriminated against, or held back from opportunities, if he or she is stuck in a dead-ended job, has a toxic supervisor, and gets all the lousy assignments, then quality of work life is low for that person.

A later chapter provides a detailed descriptive model for defining quality of work and for measuring it in terms of statistical perceptions on the part of employees. Suffice it to say here that an organization cannot possibly have a positive, success-oriented culture when quality of work life is low for a significant number of its people.

If the executives neglect to pay attention to quality of work life or have never even learned to think in those terms, they are likely to have a tough time winning the commitment and enthusiasm of the workers. The worker thinks, "You don't care about me, so why the hell should I care about you?" It becomes very difficult to establish the sense of common purpose needed for a major service-quality program when this "us and them" feeling exists on the part of the executives and the employees alike.

Worse, it is well established that negative feelings on the part of customer-contact employees tend to contaminate the moments of truth. If employees are angry, disaffected, and convinced "the company" doesn't care about them, it is very difficult for them to be cheerful, cordial, energetic, and positive in dealing with their customers. It is a fact that:

The way your employees feel is the way your customers are going to feel.

EMPLOYEE CYNICISM

Sometimes the employees of a company don't believe anything matters. Culture and climate problems, quality of work life problems, or circumstances outside the control of executive management may have made them give up on being excited. They may be feeling jaded and pessimistic about the prospect of the organization ever changing. They may have lost confidence in upper management. Or they may have lost faith in the idea that quality counts with the customer.

In the middle of an economic recession, when people are losing their jobs and management seems to have no other vocabulary but that of cost reduction, people can become discouraged and cynical about quality. When management asks them to undertake a service-quality initiative in the middle of hard times, employees may not believe it is possible, even if they believe management is sincere in its intentions.

Some health-care workers, especially those in traditional hospitals, may see themselves as in a dying industry or at least believe their part of it is dying. Structural changes in an industry, like those going on in health care, banking, and financial services, tend to be very painful for those whose specialties are in decline. No one likes to face the prospect of having to change horses and do something different for a living.

Some types of jobs have a much higher burnout factor than others. Social workers, for example, seem to experience the ruboff effects of dealing every day with people who are down and out, depressed, and have low self-esteem. Many social workers become burned out but remain convinced they are unaffected by their jobs. This can make them negative, pessimistic, and cynical in their attitudes about life, and in particular about the organizations they work for. Those who work in government bureaucracies often become especially cynical about the red tape and impersonal rigamarole they must deal with in helping people. They may be burned out, but may rationalize it by pointing to the organization as the source of their discontent.

Another group of employees who are highly susceptible to cynicism are public utility workers. The local gas and electric company is usually a convenient political goat for politicians who need attention and for newspaper reporters who need column inches. The utility can almost always be counted on to be doing something observers can criticize, either in terms of bills, rate increases, lack of conservation efforts, or lack of cost control. This makes it very difficult for employees of the utility to take pride in their company and feel good about what they do. Also, in a number of cases, executives probably deserve about 50 percent of the brickbats they're getting because of past blunders, and the employees may be understandably cynical.

Finally, if senior executives have not been paying proper attention to culture and quality of work life issues, the employees may be feeling antagonistic as well as cynical. They may have been—or believe they have been—let down, lied to, cheated, double-crossed, or exploited. When top management comes at them with another "program," it's no wonder they don't want any part of it.

EXECUTIVE CREDIBILITY PROBLEMS

A major service initiative requires strong leadership—from the top. Leadership cannot work without credibility. And credibility comes with personal integrity, not with a job title. The executive office of a corporation has no credibility attached to it. Only the person who occupies that office can have credibility in the eyes of the working people.

Two levels of executive credibility are important: credibility in the eyes of middle and line managers and credibility in the eyes of frontline workers. If either level is in jeopardy, it will be difficult for top management to exert the leadership needed to build commitment and enthusiasm and to inspire people to follow through.

When a senior executive has a low or negative credibility rating with middle managers, they tend to respond only halfheartedly to his or her ideas and direction. It becomes necessary for the executive to use formal authority, pressure, and direct orders to get them to respond. Effective management has two parts: clout and charisma. Clout is formal authority, while charisma is earned authority. An executive who has both clout and charisma can get a wholehearted response from the middle managers; one half of the "heart" is the response to authority, and the other half is response to a respected person. If credibility goes down the tubes, charisma goes down with it, leaving clout as the only means for influence.

Similarly, when frontline people like, admire, and respect their top managers, they feel compelled, at least to some extent, to support them and contribute to the direction they have established. The executives enjoy the personal commitment and loyalty of the frontline people, over and above their formal compliance. But if workers don't believe in their executives, they feel no reason to respond positively to them on a personal level. Consequently, they become passive, reluctant, and uncommitted.

Some executives lack a clear sense of themselves as public figures in their organizations. They don't fully realize that their day-to-day behavior has symbolic significance in the eyes of their subordinates. The way they talk, the way they carry themselves, the way they listen and converse, the way they give direction, all contribute to an image of respectability or disrespectability. Their personal lives and traits may also be under curious scrutiny.

An executive who breaks the rules of credibility and loses the respect of subordinates will usually find it difficult to win it back. It may take a long time. Some executives can be remarkably clumsy and unaware of credibility factors in their conduct. Some are even guilty of transgressions of moral standards. Having an affair with a subordinate, for example, and favoring that subordinate in conflicts with that person's boss can permanently damage the executive's credibility and perceived character.

Interpersonal favoritism is not the only kind that damages credibility. Having an inside group of favored executives who cater to one's ego can also be divisive. If only certain fairhaired people enjoy access to the senior executive, while the rest are left out of the power circle, managers quickly learn that political maneuvering is more important than giving leadership to their organizations.

Some executives play one person or faction against another, causing friction and animosity and damaging their credibility. Others make promises and fail to keep their word, making their subordinates feel lied to or misled. Some are punitive or vindictive, making people overly cautious and fearful about speaking up.

Sometimes executives are so preoccupied with operational and financial matters they don't seem to know or care about the important concerns of the employees. They show, by the focus of their attention, that the people issues are at the bottom of their priority lists. When the time comes that they need the support and involvement of the workers, they have nothing in the bank to rely on. When they need to ask middle managers to make sacrifices in tough times, they don't get a sympathetic response.

Some executive groups with low or negative credibility have worked long and hard to earn it. Some waffle and vacillate on important issues; their decisions seem arbitrary, unpredictable, and inconsistent, causing their subordinates to conclude they don't have what it takes to lead. People don't trust them to know how to do the right thing. When the word of the chief executive doesn't mean anything, it will be a long road to get the people turned on.

ORGANIZATIONAL ARTHRITIS

Highly structured, rule-oriented organizations typically suffer from arthritis in one form or another. Government agencies, military organizations, educational institutions, banks, insurance companies, and public utilities are all especially susceptible to the effects of fossilization. Through the fault of no one in particular, the arthritic organization has evolved to an internal state of affairs that places compliance above common sense, policy above people, rules above reason. This makes it very difficult for people to question and reexamine the ways they do things and to experiment with new ways that may be more effective.

Arthritis can take several forms. It usually involves an absolutely minimal degree of autonomy and discretion on the part of frontline employees. It often comes about because of highly "productionized," routine, repetitive work processes that condition people to a "one best way" of working and thinking. Fully conditioned, robotic frontline workers who have been in their jobs for many years may find it difficult to objectively analyze what they do. And fossilized managers, who have never been required to think originally and resourcefully, become keepers of the status quo.

In the arthritic organization, people are not authorized to think. The policies, procedures, systems, rules, decision criteria, and job descriptions have all been optimized for maximum control and minimum risk. In this kind of an organization, not doing anything wrong becomes more important than doing something right.

In fact, some organizations become so rigidly structured internally that it becomes almost impossible for significant change to originate from within. They need some outside intervention in the form of a shock of some kind, or an environmental threat, or a common enemy, or perhaps a new executive with new ideas. The rules and controls have become so self-serving that something or someone has to forcibly introduce alternatives to the current habit pattern.

Arthritic organizations tend to be their own worst enemies when it comes to significant change. Their built-in automatic responses work against doing anything differently. They may be highly performance-oriented and may be rather efficient, at least in terms of resource utilization. But their almost neurotic preoccupation with rules and controls makes it difficult for them to release the individual energies, initiative, and creativity needed at the front line to make a major impact on service quality.

MIDDLE MANAGEMENT INERTIA

One of the most recalcitrant top management issues of our time is the middle management problem. Books have been written about it, seminars have been taught about it, executives have lamented about it, and still it prevails. In countless organizations, middle managers seem to operate more as inertial resistance forces against top-down approaches than as active sources of leadership and reinforcement.

I have often heard senior executives say, in looking back over a two- or three-year span of a major program of almost any type, "If I had it to do over, I'd have done a lot more to get middle management on board. I never really felt they were with us." Or, "It seemed like the frontline employees were more excited and committed than their managers were."

A later chapter discusses this middle management syndrome in further depth. The response of middle managers can make the difference between a program that plods along and one that comes alive and proceeds with an apparent energy all its own. If middle managers buy into it, if they are excited about it, they will communicate that excitement to their subordinate managers and workers every day. If they respond bureaucratically, treating it as just another program, it will be just another program.

This lack of middle management energy tends to be very frustrating and disconcerting to senior executives who are used to action. They are accustomed to giving orders and having them followed, when dealing with concrete operational issues their subordinates understand. This is the easy part of top management. But when it comes to communicating an abstract message like service quality to and through middle managers, executives discover it's not as easy as they thought. What seems to them a simple, compelling, and exciting prospect—"we want to compete in our marketplace on the basis of top-quality service to our customers"—doesn't seem to turn the middle managers on. The message is too vague, too ethereal, too insubstantial to register with their operationally oriented habits of thought.

Organizations seem to have a "half-life of excitement" phenomenon when it comes to executives selling their ideas down through the ranks. The chief is excited and committed to a new idea that has promise. He or she takes the idea to the executive staff, and after a great deal of discussion and selling, each of them comes away about 50 percent as excited as the chief is. Each of them communicates his or her 50 percent excitement to the next level of subordinates, each of whom gets about 50 percent as excited as the boss is. And so it goes on down the line, with the excitement level diminishing by 50 percent or so at each organizational layer until it finally gets down to the noise level of all the other messages moving around in the collective organizational conscious. At that level, it means no more than anything else the employees have heard.

Quite a few senior executives, usually the less-seasoned ones, still believe that all they have to do is tell their direct-report executives or middle managers what they want to accomplish and it will somehow magically get done. They seem to believe that the standard organizational chart—the "wiring diagram" of the company—actually describes the communication processes in the organization. They have the impression that a message, once inserted into the top of the tree, will find its way undiminished and undistorted down through the various levels to reach the working person.

Unfortunately, very little finds its way down through the levels—or up, for that matter. If the boss wants a message heard, understood, and accepted at all levels, it will be necessary to communicate it at all of those levels. Assuming it will trickle down from the top, all the way through the layers of diminishing excitement and commitment, is a prescription for disappointment.

CONFLICTED VALUE SYSTEMS

Sometimes the values, traditions, beliefs, and even professional education of certain kinds of people can stand in the way of their adopting service-oriented attitudes and behavior. Some people just don't like the idea of being in a "service job." They consider service jobs to be low in status, demeaning, and lacking in respect.

There is ample justification for this conviction in western cultures. The word *service* comes from the Latin root *servus,* which meant slave. We have words like servant, servitude, and servile to describe those who are subordinate to others. Service jobs in general do not have high status in western societies. Yet, as the scientist and humanitarian Albert Schweitzer observed, "The highest thing we can do is to serve." A statement attributed to Schweitzer illustrates the depth of the values behind serving others:

> No ray of sunlight is ever lost; but the green which it awakes into existence needs time to grow, and it is not always granted to the sower to see the harvest. All work that is worth anything is done in faith.

Some people who have been highly trained for certain professions have trouble thinking of themselves as serving anybody, and especially treating anybody like a customer. This can include physicians, nurses and allied health professionals, social workers, psychologists, lawyers, police officers, and educators.

Physicians probably experience the most role conflict and status anxiety when asked to think about their customers in a different way. Hospitals that have salaried staff physicians and health maintenance organization (HMO) groups have tried to enlist the support of their doctors in creating customer-oriented operations in health care, generally with minimal results. Doctors have been so revered and catered to in American-style fee-for-service medicine that they have enjoyed an exalted social and professional status. For a doctor to talk to a patient as if that person were a customer, i.e., one who pays for a product and is entitled to get his money's worth, is largely unthinkable.

The health-care industry has developed, over the years, a remarkable set of tactics for making its customers feel psychologically subordinate and deferential toward the care-givers. One of the most sacred of these rules is to never refer to the customer as a customer, but rather as a patient. A customer is someone who buys something; a patient is someone who comes seeking relief from some discomfort and finds it in the hands of the expert caregiver. The fact that money changes hands is somehow irrelevant to the relationship.

It is interesting to see medical people of various kinds trying to cope with the new reality in the health-care business. Many of them are extremely distressed about the "commercialization of American medicine." They can't bear the thought of calling the patient a customer.

Nurses in hospitals often experience the same kinds of role conflict as doctors, although there is less risk of loss of status for them. Many nurses feel comfortable with the idea of giving quality care, but the idea of treating the patient as a customer is something else. They find the idea of putting the customer in the driver's seat as vaguely repulsive. Those who have this kind of value-system conflict often have trouble participating in a service-quality program launched by hospital management.

The terminology often tells a tale. Margaret McGee, my business manager, reports hearing a technician in an X-ray department refer to a special apparatus for X-raying small children as a "bratboard." Some physicians find it more convenient to talk in terms of the gall bladder in 2210, or the interesting kidney on the third floor, than in terms of the people who own the organs under discussion.

Psychologists and social workers often have the same kinds of conflicting value systems with respect to their customers. They have evolved the term *client* to denote the person they do business with; *customer* just seems too crass.

Lawyers are in much the same boat as doctors. The oversupply of lawyers in most urban markets and the removal of restrictions on advertising and promotion have forced many of them to compete for business more overtly and aggressively. Larger law firms that are adopting the service management model for their businesses need to make the idea of customer orientation palatable to lawyers who have been raised to see people as clients.

Police officers are in a peculiar position, and many of them are experiencing the pressure of rethinking their relationships to the community. Police work is a service, but it is difficult to treat someone like a customer when that someone is acting like a crook. Police officers who constantly deal with the public typically experience very difficult role conflicts. In dealing with the majority of reputable citizens, they are expected to be polite, courteous, and service oriented. In dealing with the smaller but more contentious segment of the population, they are expected to be assertive, commanding, and even violent when necessary.

Having to switch suddenly and without warning from one of these two contrasting psychological configurations to the other is very demanding. It takes its toll in stress, quality of life, and even psychological adjustment for many of them. Yet it is becoming clear that police organizations must maintain high-quality relationships with various sectors of the community in order to preserve order and to carry out their jobs when public order is in question.

Educators may be the last people to adopt a service orientation toward the people they are supposed to serve. The educational systems in the western world have been in the hands of governments for so long that they have become like most other government services—bureaucratized and institutionalized. To suggest that the learners, and those paying for the education the learners are supposed to receive, are *customers* draws a blank look from traditional educators. Those who take this unusual attitude are vastly outnumbered by those who think of the educational institution as a permanent fixture and the students as merely passers-by who flow through the system and leave money behind.

In all of these cases, when the value systems that come into play are in direct conflict, it is difficult for the people involved to put their hearts and souls into any kind of service program. The leaders of any organization with its values in a state of conflict will first have to resolve the value conflicts, or at least find a compromise ground where the psychological needs of the servers can be compatible with the service strategy of the organization.

MISALIGNED INCENTIVES

In the language of the "pop-psych" theory of Transactional Analysis that was popular in the early 1970s:

What you stroke is what you get.

This means that people in organizations respond to the reality of the rewards and sanctions they experience, not to idealized appeals from management. If the rewards and sanctions that prevail are congruent with the service concept, then people will work in service-oriented ways. If not, they will work in ways that respond successfully—to them—to the rewards and sanctions.

The reward systems in many organizations are substantially out of whack with respect to the kinds of behavior top management is hoping to see on the part of the employees. Influences in the day-to-day work experience may operate to push people away from a service orientation rather than toward it. Some of these influences come directly from management; others come from the operational priorities that are in place. Middle and junior managers notice who gets fed and who gets flogged and for what apparent reasons. They quickly learn to do what gets them fed—psychically as well as economically—and avoid doing what gets them flogged.

One of the most common counterincentives to a service orientation is the P&L whip. When the P&Ls—profit and loss statements—occupy center stage in the corporate consciousness, everything else takes a back seat. When hotel managers, store managers, restaurant managers, and others with P&L responsibility hear only the language of finance from their bosses, they quickly learn that financial performance is the starting point rather than the ending point for consideration of product quality. When the P&L whip comes out, it often has the effect of contradicting everything previously said about customer service, customer satisfaction, and the like. One message is ideal; the other is real.

This perceived quality-cost conflict plagues the executives of many service businesses, and they have great difficulty resolving it. It is important to portray the priorities of cost consciousness and cost control, and even cost reductions, as falling within the overall service quality thrust, not as contradicting it. A later chapter describes methods for reconciling the realities of cost reduction with a service focus.

Another source of conflicting incentives is the production versus quality syndrome. In production-oriented service businesses, where the service product is highly routinized and measurable, operating priorities tend to drift toward production efficiency and away from the softer, less distinct focus of value to the customer. This syndrome has unfortunately befallen AT&T, once known for its service and customer-mindedness. AT&T operators have, in most cases, been horsewhipped to meet production standards aimed at minimizing labor costs per call. As a result, many of them have become fully robotized and disenchanted with their jobs. Customers immediately experience the negative feelings and "don't care" attitude, which was rare in the "old" AT&T.

Another, more disturbing case of the production-quality conflict is in many HMOs. A fairly representative example is the Kaiser Permanente plan, which operates a large system of hospitals in California and the western United States. The doctors in this system are on a salary-based compensation arrangement, working as employees of a physician's association that contracts with the HMO company for their services. Consequently, they do not have the same financial motivations that bear upon their private-practice counterparts who make more money by treating more patients.

In a system like this—which has been typical in most European countries for years—the salaried physician is expected to see a certain number of patients per shift. Because of this "unionized" means of delivering medical care, HMO doctors have little incentive to see more patients or to spend extra time with a patient who needs a bit of counselling or assurance. It's a "get 'em in and get 'em out" type of system. The result is long waiting periods for customers who need to schedule appointments. Whereas the receptionists of private-practice doctors almost always seem to be able to "fit you in," HMO scheduling people seldom do.

To add the finishing touch to a system that is programmed for mediocrity, large HMO systems like Kaiser practice aggressive forms of "utilization control," which is a process of screening patients to minimize the number who get through the system for treatment by the more expensive specialists and costly procedures. Family practice doctors in most of these systems are the screeners. Their job is to review the patient's condition and treat it if possible. Only if they believe it is essential do they refer the patient into the treatment system.

Many physicians in these kinds of organizational systems are committed to high personal standards of medical practice and personal service to their customers. But some are not, and these tend to be the ones who drift into the production mode, which unfortunately contributes to the image of "factory medicine" on the part of such organizations.

Just as with the profit-quality conflict, the production-quality conflict does not have to be irreconcilable. It is possible to make trade-offs to gain efficiencies of cost and resource control. But the key is to make the trade-offs within a framework that makes service quality the driving organizational priority, not the residue of a cost-minded control mentality.

GAMING

A service quality program can sink, starve, or wither on the vine if it becomes the focus of conflict and game playing between factions in the organization. Most chief executives learn, often to their dismay, that power and authority have their limits. There are boundaries to the efficacy of command. The executive function can bid people to behave or not to behave in certain specific ways, but it cannot oblige them to feel a certain way.

In one organization I worked with, top management fell into an unfortunate game with the middle managers and department heads. Overestimating the climate and degree of readiness of the managers to embrace a service initiative, we launched a service management program from the top. Although the frontline employees were overwhelmingly enthusiastic about the possibilities of the new venture, the department heads were underwhelmed. A number of them adopted a passive resistance strategy, doing little or nothing to carry the message of the program to the working people.

In conversations with executives, a number of department heads referred to the venture as "your service management program," meaning it belonged psychologically to upper management. It was a time of turmoil in the organization as well as its industry; resources were tight and getting tighter. Part of the gaming dynamic involved department heads saying, "How can you expect me to do your service management program when you won't give me any more resources? If you'll give me more staff, I can give you better service." This reaction, which I have seen a number of times before and since, seems to rest on the unspoken supposition that there exists somewhere a figurative price list for service. It's as if each element of service quality carries a separate price tag, and you can buy additional increments of service quality by deciding how much money you want to put up for it.

The hole we fell into during that implementation was assuming that the vision behind the program would be as compelling for the middle managers as it was for senior management and frontline employees. Unfortunately, a number of the middle managers had private agendas of their own in the situation and elected to use the service program as a way to game their superiors and pay them back for cutting their budgets. They never even mentioned the program to their subordinates; they acted as if it didn't exist. The result was that the subordinates got confusing and conflicting messages and weren't sure whether the program really was important to the organization.

A service program can also become a political football if one department, such as marketing, has all the responsibility for carrying it out. If any other departments have been involved in gamy relationships with the advocating department in the past, then the service program can supply more ammunition for the battle. The venture becomes "their" program, and "they are trying to push it down our throats."

There can be a great deal of special-interest or special-issue gaming going on as well. Field organizations may use the new program as a forum for asserting their demands or airing their complaints. Affinity groups such as nurses in hospitals, flight attendants in airlines, and union groups of all types may be tempted to retaliate at upper management by passively sabotaging a new program if they sense that upper management has a strong psychological investment in it.

Top management can end up in the awkward position of demanding compliance and exhorting factional leaders to lend their support, but not being able to define in so many words what they should actually do. Without a middle management buy-in, top managers know they're being gamed, but don't know how to deal with it. Power and authority can instill fear and literal obedience, but it cannot instill commitment.

Sometimes a top management group will resort to gaming the middle managers in a frustrated attempt to get them to carry out a program. One method is simply to promise a certain thing in the advertisements to the customers, and let the customers put the heat on the service people to deliver. One major high-luxury hotel chain had trouble getting food and beverage managers to serve fresh-squeezed orange juice. So they simply started advertising it to the customers. The result was a rise in customer complaints and a great deal of exasperation at the field levels, not a greater commitment or enthusiasm for service.

The executives of another organization, a large grocery chain, fell into the same trap, but by accident rather than design. They advertised to their customers "Three's enough." This meant that, whenever a checkout line had more than three customers waiting, the store manager would open up another line, even if he or she had to operate the register.

Unfortunately, they forgot to let their store managers in on the new plan before they told the customers about it. In one store, the lines got longer than the adverts said they should, and the customers started calling for more checkers. Somebody shouted, "Three's enough." The other customers took up the slogan, and soon everybody in the checkout area was chanting, "Three's enough! Three's enough! Three's enough!" The checkers and the store managers were baffled. The customers had seen the ads, but the employees hadn't.

In a southern California hospital, executives decided all of the nurses should have college degrees. So they informed all the nurses that they were terminated as of a certain date, and those who had degrees or were actively pursuing degrees could have their positions back. Sounds like a real morale-builder, doesn't it?

Gaming may result from an ambitious program launch that doesn't win the support, involvement, and commitment of the important factional interests at the outset. If the actions of middle managers, special interest representatives, and union leaders are critical to the success of the program, then a special effort, very early in the process, is needed to establish a basis for their buy-in.

HEADQUARTERS–FIELD CONFLICT

In the case of organizations that employ a number of local outlets to deliver their services, such as hotel chains, restaurant chains, drug and convenience store chains, national brokerage firms, national insurance firms, and the like, the age-old conflict between headquarters and the field can sometimes block the way. There is hardly a regionalized organization to be found in which headquarters people don't feel that field people ignore or resist guidance, and in which field people don't feel that headquarters people are out of touch with reality and preoccupied with irrelevant matters. It just seems to be in the nature of the beast.

In some organizations, the relationship between headquarters and the field may be cooperative and constructive, while in others it may be highly antagonistic. If field people criticize and complain about almost everything "the ivory tower" does, there will be a dangerous precedent in place for bad-mouthing any new initiative for service quality. Conversely, headquarters people may approach the new venture with the assumption that field people won't want to do it and will resist it "the way they fight everything else." In such a climate, the program is set up for failure at the outset.

The resistance of field managers can take a number of forms. One form is the "we're different" point of view. "We're in Pocatello, (or Portland or Poughkeepsie) and our situation is different. This shouldn't apply to us." Another reaction is the "you first" ploy. Field managers can nearly always point to some area in which headquarters has messed up and say, "You should get your own act together first; you're the cause of most of the service problems. When you get headquarters straightened out, then we can do our part." That one is guaranteed to get them a 25-year reprieve from having to implement any new program from headquarters. And sometimes it's just the plain old "NIH" syndrome—Not Invented Here.

Field people may feel defensive about any new program that suggests they don't already give good service. They may be tempted to rationalize away market research data that might indicate the quality of service needs improving. Sometimes a service initiative that top management believes has the potential of elevating service quality to customer-pleasing levels can look to field managers like a put-down to the field.

With regard to all of the potential pitfalls just enumerated, it is important for top management to understand the present climate in the organization before undertaking a major service quality program. It is also crucially important to presell the idea of the program and its potential benefits to the key action people, and to avoid springing it on them without warning or time for preparation. The more positive atmosphere that will prevail offers benefits that usually far outweigh the drawbacks of a slower, more deliberate start.

CHAPTER 6

"GENERAL MOTORS" MANAGEMENT DOESN'T WORK FOR SERVICE

We trained hard—but it seemed that every time we were beginning to form up into teams, we would be reorganized. I was to learn later in life that we tend to meet any new situation by reorganization, and a wonderful method it can be for creating the illusion of progress while producing confusion, inefficiency, and demoralization.

—*Petronius Arbiter*

THE MANUFACTURING MODEL HAS FAILED

For a number of years we have been trying to use the methods and precepts of *manufacturing* management to run *service* businesses, and it hasn't been working very well. As service organizations have become larger and more diversified, the old manufacturing-oriented thinking has become more of an obstacle than a resource. The "General Motors" model is becoming more and more clearly inappropriate for the delivery of high-quality moments of truth. When I use the term *General Motors management*, I do not mean to imply anything disparaging about General Motors. I am merely coining a metaphor—a form of intellectual shorthand for describing a point of view about organizations.

Most managers in western countries have been educated to a management theory that is manufacturing oriented in its basic worldview. This manufacturing paradigm, which arose in the early part of this century, is so prevalent in western thought that there has been no serious competitor to it over these many years. Managers who attend business school courses, in-company training programs, or public seminars all get much the same philosophy. Those who learn the ropes by working under other managers tend to pick up the philosophy more or less unconsciously as if by osmosis.

And when it comes time to think about the nature and operation of service businesses, whether they are brokerage firms or hamburger chains, the General Motors thinking process tends to prevail. The organizational structures, functional subdivisions, allocations of authority, and deployment of resources tend to fall into place according to a traditional structuring motif centered on control and regulation.

What I am calling the GM model of management literally had its origins with General Motors. During World War II, GM had to take on the task of producing a tremendous number of vehicles of various types for the war effort. To do this, the company had to expand its operations radically. We must remember that, up until that time, there were no super-large companies in existence. The existence of companies with several hundred thousand employees is distinctly a postwar phenomenon. IBM, Exxon, Boeing and the other aerospace giants, and AT&T did not exist in anything like their present form. During the years of its phenomenal physical growth under the leadership of Alfred P. Sloan, GM had to solve the unprecedented problems of bigness.[1]

During that period, Austrian-born management consultant Peter F. Drucker got involved with GM as adviser and observer. For several years, he roamed about in the organization, studying the problems managers were experiencing and observing the solutions top management worked out for the problems of size and growth. Issues like the definition of mission and direction, centralization versus decentralization of responsibility and authority, coordination of activities between operating divisions, and development of professional managers drew his attention. Drucker admired many of the solutions GM evolved. His observations became the substance of his landmark book *The Concept of the Corporation*.[2]

Drucker's ideas, in that and subsequent books, had such a strong impact on senior managers that General Motors became for many the primary point of reference for thinking about their own organizations. For at least 30 years, Drucker and GM were almost symbolic of the gospel of corporate management. For all of that time, Drucker has been the most widely read and quoted of all management theorists in the United States, and probably the world. Virtually all of his 24 books have been business best-sellers, and he has been the acknowledged dean of management theorists.

And now, as American society has passed out of the Industrial Age and into the Information Age and western economies have shifted from a manufacturing structure to a service structure, General Motors is no longer the unquestioned management model of choice. And Drucker, of course, always the consummate visionary, was one of the first to recognize this. In an interview with *Business Week* magazine, he explained why GM is no longer the definitive model:

> In those days it was the only model that had systematically and purposely tried to think through basic management issues. The telephone company was a monopoly. And General Electric was a mess. Today there is no one model anymore. The flagships of the past, large institutions like General Motors and ITT, have basically outlived their usefulness. A penalty of size is that you try to do everything, and no one can do everything well.[3]

Drucker doesn't seem to have a new model to propose. Even General Motors seems to be trying to find a new model. It's as if the executives of Old Reliable are trying to undo some of the things they've spent decades doing. Like so many mega-organizations, GM seems to be at war with itself. A recent image ad published by the company in *The New Yorker* tries to convey an impression of a new way of thinking about making cars and trucks. Titles like "How to Run a Factory without Any Neckties" and "Let the People Participate in Managing the Business" are old stuff from the point of view of alternative management thinking, but still pretty fancy for a manufacturing culture like GM.

So here we are, late in the 20th century, with a service-oriented economy and a manufacturing-oriented management paradigm. Evolving a new management paradigm will take some time. It will take even longer for it to displace the current GM model as the dominant motif in western management thought. This chapter will highlight a few key features that must be a part of the new paradigm and suggest some ways corporations can begin to revolutionize—or evolutionize—their business models.

THE END OF THE ROAD FOR THE
HARVARD GOSPEL?

If General Motors and Peter Drucker have been the prophets of American management technique, surely the Harvard Business School has been its high church. Harvard and several other prestigious biz-schools like the University of Pennsylvania's Wharton School, MIT's Sloan School of Business, Stanford University, and the University of Southern California have for three or four decades trained and indoctrinated budding young professionals and seasoned executives alike in the doctrine of GM management. What has come to be known as "The Gospel According to the Harvard Business School" is a clear set of precepts about the management of organizations for profit.[4]

What I refer to here as the Harvard gospel is a thinking process, a point of view about organizations, and an analytical model for deciding what to do with organizations. It has led many an organization out of the wilderness and into the land of profitability. It has served as a powerful intellectual framework for American business and business in many other countries. When we talk about its obsolescence with respect to the management of service businesses, we must be careful not to throw out the baby with the bath water. Any replacement paradigm will have to offer solutions to most of the problems the Harvard gospel solves, as well as provide a shift in focus. We must give credit where it is due, and not fall for the temptation to try to sweep aside the intellectual legacy of the past three or four decades as if it were no longer valid in any way.

But it is important to recognize the elements of the traditional Harvard management model that may no longer apply in the context of service. Let's quickly trace the reasoning process that underlies the Harvard/GM approach to organizational thinking and try to pinpoint the structures that need changing.

The Harvard model, as I see it, represents the corporation as a fundamentally economic entity. It is a construct derived from the assembly of capital and the application of labor to produce a product that will sell in a marketplace. According to the doctrine, you proceed roughly as follows. First, you define the market, or the business, you want to be in. This includes at least a general definition of the product you plan to market. Then you define the organization needed to implement the product. You establish strategy, set objectives, define organizational functions that must be performed to get the product to the market, and subdivide the organization into its basic components.

Once you have the organization roughly laid out, you proceed to define its structure in great detail. You break divisions into departments, departments into branches, branches into sections, and finally sections into individual work units. This subdivision, of course, varies considerably with the type of organization and the work to be done. When you have specified the smallest organizational unit, the next step is to define individual jobs, one per person. For each job—theoretically, at least—you write a job description, which is a specification that tells any person who might occupy that job exactly how to do it. You might also define specific job standards, which are concrete measures of performance on certain key job tasks.

Once you have all of this defined, according to the Harvard doctrine, you then go and get some workers and plug them into the jobs. Note that definition comes first and people follow. Management, then, becomes the process of seeing to it that the people do the jobs they're supposed to do. The Harvard model is essentially an inhuman model, i.e., the focus of thought is on structure rather than people. The language of business-school courses is largely the language of finance, with case studies as one of the primary learning methods. Courses deal largely with organizational theory, finance and accounting, strategy, marketing methods, policy, management systems, and an occasional course in personnel. Most MBA programs in the United States tend toward a financial concentration. The "fresh young MBAs" so often mentioned in magazine articles are typically accountants.

Almost every MBA program has one or more token courses dealing with the human element, i.e., human behavior, organizational behavior, and motivation. In rare cases, there may be a course on creativity. But most programs are overlaid on a basic educational substrate that treats the business as a technical-economic structure. This econometric approach gives rise to the much-vaunted *bottom line* orientation so prevalent in western business. The balance sheet and income statement become the prayer books and hymnals in the worship of profit.

In the management of service businesses, the Harvard gospel is not so much incorrect as it is inappropriate in its intellectual focus. The conceptualization of the organization as a strictly economic entity, and the view that productivity of capital and labor is the appropriate focus for management, leads to a nonhuman view of what is essentially a human process. The Harvard gospel lacks any significant conceptual structure that allows for a focus on people as the key to market success. In reality, the people are the capital, the labor, and the product, all rolled into one. They are an asset that appreciates in value, and this is a concept no accounting model has yet managed to incorporate.

THE GHOST OF FREDERICK TAYLOR WALKS THE LAND

Actually, the Harvard/GM school of structural management originated largely from the thought processes of one man more than any other. That man was Frederick Winslow Taylor, one of the first management consultants, who operated early in this century. Taylor was the father of the work analysis methods that underlie most of what today goes by the name of industrial engineering. His methods became the basis of much of modern management practice, at least so far as tactical work-level supervision is concerned.

He realized that work efficiency and productivity would be extremely important, and he concluded that the low skills and minimal education of the workers would require some form of simplification and standardization of the work for them. Taylor believed that, for every job, there was "one best way" for the worker to do the work. His concept of scientific management called for technical experts like him to analyze every job in detail, break it down into its smallest movements, and rearrange the movements to minimize wasted energy. Once management determined the one best way for the job, it remained only to teach the method to the worker and make sure he followed it.

Taylor's studies proved, for example, that a worker doing heavy manual labor could accomplish more in a day if allowed to rest periodically than if he had to keep moving. Many managers who saw Taylor's methods in action became very impressed with the results. His book *The Principles of Scientific Management* set forth his methods in a very readable way.[5]

Taylor's approach seemed like the answer to many management problems during the early and middle years of the Industrial Revolution. His work analysis perspective became such a dominant paradigm that it, plus the top-management perspective brought later by Drucker and General Motors, *became* management in most western countries. It led to the work of Frank and Lillian Gilbreth, who made the term *efficiency expert* part of the American language. Gilbreth, whose life and work formed the basis of the movie "Cheaper by the Dozen," perfected the methods of time-and-motion studies and helped many businesses organize their manufacturing processes.

Gilbreth's contribution gained such wide respect that industrial engineers coined the term *therblig,* a reversal of the spelling of his name, to describe the smallest observable motor action of a job. Typical therbligs were reach, grasp, move, insert, turn, fold, and bend. Many industrial engineers still speak of therbligs in analyzing work processes. And many managers, even though they have never heard the term, still analyze jobs the same way. Unfortunately, in service businesses, we're still thinking in terms of therbligs rather than moments of truth.

The contributions of Frederick Taylor and his followers have been enormously influential in shaping western management philosophy and practice. But we have entered an age where the manufacturing model is no longer the operative reality, and it is time to replace parts of the Tayloristic approach with new ways of thinking that recognize the personal and interpersonal character of service work.

History makes it clear that the process by which a new paradigm displaces an established one is usually confusing, unsettling, and messy. And, of course, it is only a conjecture that this is indeed what is underway as the service revolution proceeds. A paradigm shift takes time, causes pain, and eventually offers benefits superior to those offered by the old paradigm, or else the shift never happens.

We're not ready to expunge Taylor's name from the management history books by any means. The man's shadow stretches across some 60 to 70 years of history; his ghost still walks the land. His ideas and methods still dominate most of western management thought, and parts of his philosophy are still valid. But we are still tool-and-task oriented; still structure oriented; still oriented to process and procedure rather than to human interaction. In a service management environment, we need to think in terms of workers having transactions with the customer, rather than in terms of workers performing predefined tasks. And the Taylor/GM model has little to offer for enlightening our understanding of the customer interface.

MANAGEMENT NEUROSES

One of Peter Drucker's most insightful comments was, "Much of what we call management consists of making it difficult for people to get their work done." When I think about the management jobs I've held, ranging from military officer to R&D program manager, to new-product development manager, and as an owner of small businesses, I realize that much of what I considered management involved serving my own needs to feel in charge. Some of my ideas about direction, visibility, and control were really part of what I have come to call the neuroses of management.

The GM approach to management impels managers to "know what's going on." They must "be on top of things." They must not "let things get out of hand." Yet it is arguable in many cases whether the rules, controls, and reporting processes imposed on working people by managers really contribute to organizational performance. Or do they just make managers feel powerful and secure? Might they actually be wasting time and energy on the part of the workers that might go to more productive use?

The neuroses of management can even spill over into the manager's personal life. When I was married, I remember establishing firm rules for the household about watching expenditures. I demanded detailed records, showing income and expenditures in various categories. My wife, I later realized, had the cash flow situation well under control and had no need of my "reports." And I seldom looked at them anyway. So eventually she stopped keeping the information, and she discovered she could produce whatever figures I asked for in my sporadic episodes of control anxiety.

There is a near-paranoid fear on the part of many managers about not knowing what is going on and about allowing workers too much freedom. One of the powerful appeals of the Taylor/GM model of management seems to be that it caters to the appetite that exists in so many managers for control and certainty. *Things* are easier to measure and manage than *people,* and the task-structure-process approach makes managers feel good.

Yet it is becoming clear that the GM model brings with it certain side effects that are very difficult to fix. In service environments, the model typically leads to overdirection, overcontrol, and constant demands for status reporting. These management neuroses, and the kind of work climate they create, can stand in the way of mobilizing the best efforts of frontline workers, who are operating at the moments of truth. There seems to be a mind-set that favors system solutions over people solutions.

Another element of the management neurosis is the need to feel and display power from time to time, power in its elemental form, power for its own sake. Sometimes managers become so intent on making sure everybody knows who is in charge that they create rules and regulations, policies, restrictions, and punishment systems that make the organization resemble a prison more than a business operation.

News Item: "A ban on non-designer jeans has been lifted from the dress code for air traffic controllers at the Los Angeles Air Traffic Control Center in Palmdale, the Federal Aviation Administration said. The dress code instituted by the center in May restricted the brands of jeans that could be worn to the Calvin Klein, Jordache, Sergio Valente and Gloria Vanderbilt designer labels. All other brands, as well as any jeans that were faded or tattered, were banned. The rule was abandoned because of 'very strong reactions' by the 433 employees at Palmdale, said an FAA spokesman."[6]

What the dispute was about, of course, was not the wearing of jeans; it was about power. It was a pushing contest between managers who wanted to show they were in charge and the ant army who wanted to show they couldn't be rousted around. The ant army won. This kind of conflict is one of the more unfortunate side effects of the management neuroses that can arise when people misapply the philosophy of the GM approach.

There are five fundamental problems of 20th-century business that managers complain about over and over. I have come to believe these problems are consequences of—rather than afflictions suffered by—the GM philosophy of management. They are:

The motivation problem.

The productivity problem.

The performance appraisal problem.

The union problem.

The middle management problem.

The following sections discuss each of them. By looking at each of these problems from the standpoint of service businesses, we can see where the GM management thinking process leaves off and the service management thinking process must take up.

THE MOTIVATION PROBLEM

The motivation problem is becoming particularly critical now as we deal with service quality as an organizational issue. To draw a simple contrast, administering an injection to a patient in a hospital is a profoundly different type of work from assembling a carburetor in a factory. The employee who assembles the carburetor can despise carburetors, can dislike the job intensely, can be alienated from his or her work group, and can feel deeply resentful toward management and the company. Yet, if he or she simply follows the task instructions to the letter, the carburetor will come out all right and the customer will never know or care who put it together. Apart from the side effects on productivity and labor strife and the humanitarian considerations of quality of work life, the feelings and motivations of the worker have little or no impact on the perceptions of the customer.

But the nurse or technician who inserts a syringe into someone's arm is in a very different situation. He or she is interacting with the customer directly, and this moment of truth is just as much a psychological event as a physical event. The patient is very closely attuned to the personal interaction. If the nurse is angry, frustrated, burned out, turned off about the job, exasperated with hospital management, or feeling disadvantaged in quality of work life, it will be next to impossible for him or her to maintain a high level of energy, optimism, and cheerfulness in dealing with patients. It's just not normal; the negative feelings will come through sooner or later.

Executives and managers have had to invent many different techniques to try to offset the lack of a motivational theme within the GM model. They have pasted one fix after another on top of the GM methodology, not realizing that the underlying assumptions of the model itself have created the motivation problem.

For the service management approach to work in most organizations, it will probably be necessary for executives to rethink the psychological relationship between supervisor and employee because it is becoming more painfully clear all the time that it affects the quality of the psychological relationship between the employee and the customer.

THE PRODUCTIVITY PROBLEM

In New York's garment district, there was an older man who had worked for the same garment factory for 30 years. He had never missed a single day of work in all that time, nor had he ever been late—not once. All of his co-workers admired his dedication and reliability. But one day, at 9 A.M., he didn't show up as he always had. Nine-fifteen. Nine-thirty. He still wasn't there. Everyone started wondering and talking. "What do you think happened to Stanley? Where can he be?" Nine-forty-five and still no Stanley.

Finally, at 9:55 Stanley staggered in, bruised, tattered, and shaken. His co-workers immediately gathered around to comfort him. "What happened to you?" they asked.

Stanley sat down to catch his breath. "I fell down four flights of stairs. Almost got killed." The boss, who had just walked in, said sternly, "And this took you an hour?"

The productivity problem is an extension of the motivation problem: how to get more work out of people. I still see brochures promoting seminars that promise to help managers "Get more work out of your people." Titles like "Managing for Productivity" still catch the interest of many managers.

Productivity as a business issue waxes and wanes over the years, largely with the state of the economy. From about 1975 through 1982, productivity talk was in the air. Articles in business and financial magazines talked about the crisis in American productivity, about how America's rate of increase in industrial productivity was lower than that of other competitor nations and perhaps even declining. Almost every industry association conference had to have improving productivity as its theme. Articles and books on the subject proliferated. The seminar industry offered management workshops aimed at showing managers how to boost productivity.

Lately, American productivity has been rising more rapidly, in part because of an economic boom that has been taxing industrial capacity, so the productivity problem is relatively quiet. But it is still there, in the weeds, and it rears its head periodically.

The productivity problem—if there is one—is, like the motivation problem, a direct effect of the mind-set underlying the GM model of management. When all of the expectations in a situation tell employees they must simply do what they are told, they tend to do so—and no more. Because managers are then the only legitimate originators of the productivity impulse, workers are virtually always underutilized. The GM approach tries to extract performance, rather than to invite contribution.

The real productivity problem in western business economies is in the nonmanufacturing sector. Jobs involving white-collar work, over-the-counter work, information processing work, and the like, outnumber manufacturing jobs by a wide margin. If we're looking for ways to enhance productivity, it would make sense to start there. Unfortunately, these jobs do not lend themselves easily to analysis and quantification. Many service jobs are characterized not by the frequency or speed of a person's motor activities, but by the perceived value of the outcome he or she creates in the eyes of the customer.

As in the case of the motivation problem, executives and managers have tried many things to enhance productivity. In the early years, work simplification was the primary mode. Then came automation and the attempt to displace labor with sophisticated capital. Finally, we came to the get-more-work-out-of-them phase. Productivity improvement campaigns became the order of the day.

Some of these were offers to trade money for performance through gain-sharing programs like the Scanlon plan; others were attempts to motivate and excite people to produce more for the same wages. Of course, there were many union battles along the way.

Sometimes we go to great lengths to get employees to behave in certain ways when it might be easier and more effective just to approach them directly. Many of the blunders made by managers in the name of productivity have occurred because of the unconscious assumption in the GM model that people are not entitled to a psychological stake in the success of the enterprise. They are interchangeable parts in an apparatus, not participants in a human experience.

In the new age of service, the traditional GM concept of productivity is less and less valid. Although some service jobs may lend themselves to a productionized approach to defining quality, more and more of them require that we define quality in terms of outcomes rather than inputs. Job tasks and quantifiable measures of motor activity become much less important than qualitative results definable in terms of customer satisfaction.

THE PERFORMANCE APPRAISAL PROBLEM

In the information age, and with the rise of knowledge work, fewer employees have therblig-type jobs. In the United States, fewer than 18 percent of workers manufacture things. The rest of them work with information, services, or the soft kinds of jobs that do not lend themselves to mechanistic measurement. When therbligs were in, it became a fairly simple matter to determine how well a particular employee was doing his or her job. The job always had an output—a tangible thing or event. All we had to do was count the number of acceptable widgets the employee produced during the work shift and compare that to the production of the other workers. We had very clear norms for production.

In those days, performance appraisal was production appraisal. Managers and personnel officers could keep records on the fitness of the various workers and could decide how to compensate them accordingly. As with so many of the features of the GM model, this measurement motif has carried over unchanged to the service era. Many organizations are still trying to measure service work by analyzing therbligs and counting widgets. But the therbligs and widgets don't make sense any more.

What are the therbligs in a physician's diagnosis of a disorder, or when a loan officer persuades a customer to place a loan with his or her bank, or when a stockbroker advises an investor how to arrange a tax shelter, or when a travel agent shows a client how to get the lowest fare on an airplane ticket? And does it make sense to count the outputs? A service worker typically handles the moments of truth that come his or her way. If the customer doesn't come in, there is no "production" to count.

I have seen very few nonmanufacturing organizations in which the managers believed they had a workable and useful performance appraisal system. Most of these systems include all-but-useless descriptors like punctuality, attitude, grooming, initiative, cooperation, quality of work, and quantity of work.

Performance appraisal becomes nothing more than an annual bother, a ritual in which the personnel department nags the managers to "get their forms in." Managers sit down with subordinates for a few awkward minutes, they chat and socialize, and they both sign the form; it goes back to personnel and they go back to work. Typically, there is very little meaningful thought or discussion that is helpful to employee or manager. The appraisal meeting is usually an uncomfortable ritual that both would rather skip. The form is typically a formality that seldom serves any significant purpose. And the process typically has little real meaning for workers, managers, or the organization.

If we're going to make sense out of human performance in service organizations, we will have to come up with a more intelligent way of looking at it than therbligs and widgets. A later chapter advances the notion of *contribution* as a substitute for task performance in thinking about employee effectiveness. In this, as well as other ways, we will need to loosen the grip of the Taylor/ GM thinking process and look at it from a more fundamental perspective.

THE UNION PROBLEM

The union is a problem only to the management of the company. To the employees it is a solution. If you listen to a person who started work life as a professional and rose through the ranks to become a manager, you will probably hear unions and union leaders described as if they are evil forces to be eliminated. The union is the adversary, a selfish, unreasonable, uncooperative obstacle to the success of the business. The union is a problem to be dealt with. The union leaders are opponents to be outwitted.

But to the employees, at least in most unionized organizations, the union is on their side. Many workers feel the union is the only way they can get a fair shake. Their faith in top management's intentions is so low that they have chosen to have a third party represent their interests in what they perceive to be a power struggle with an impersonal, uncaring, profit-motivated in-group that is in complete control of their destinies. When you listen to a person who has spent all of his or her working life at the rank-and-file level, you will probably hear "the company" described as if it is a group of bigwigs who care only about power and profit.

Both sides may be accurate in some of their perceptions, and both are usually wrong in many ways. But it is clear that heavy unionization in an industry or a business is most often a consequence of the impersonal Taylor/GM thinking process. The Taylor/GM model didn't cause unions—the union movement had been underway for many years. But it probably did solidify the adversarial relationship in the minds of many managers, and consequently in the minds of many union leaders.

There are some large and profitable corporations that are not unionized, and not for lack of effort on the part of major unions. Eastman Kodak, for example, has long been a nonunion company in most of its operations. The Mars Company, maker of 5 out of the 10 best-selling candy bars and chocolate products in the United States, is a family-owned business that has made unionization impossible for many years, in an industry that is traditionally unionized. The managements of these companies have worked hard to prevent situations that tend to lead to formation of employee unions. Conversely, it is often the case, though not always, that a union organizing effort is the result of faulty executive leadership.

Actually, the American business sector is not nearly as heavily unionized as those of many other western countries. The Scandinavian countries, Norway, Sweden, and Denmark, are, for all practical purposes, completely unionized. Even managers in those countries have unions. Similarly, Germany, England, and Australia are heavily unionized. In contrast, the American work force has never been more than 25 to 30 percent unionized, even during times of extreme labor shortage.

Nor is American labor politics nearly so combative and vitriolic as that of, say, Australia, where workers will often strike merely to register opposition to some government policy that is completely unrelated to wages, hours, or conditions of work. In 1983, when Australia won the America's Cup race, Prime Minister Bob Hawke, who is also head of the Labor Party, commented in a nationally televised interview, "Any boss who sacks a worker for taking tomorrow off is a bum." Guess what happened the next day?

In a service business, where the climate of the organization can have an important influence on the treatment the customer receives, it is critically important that there be reasonably peaceful relations between management and workers. An indifferent, oppressive, or exploitive management style is not likely to earn the kind of employee support and commitment needed to make a service initiative succeed.

When Scandinavian Airlines President Jan Carlzon launched his unprecedented service program in that company, he called a meeting of about 120 senior managers from all over the system. He also invited about 30 key union leaders to attend. He said to them, "We're all in this together. We must find a way to turn this company into a customer-oriented business, and quickly. We can't afford to fight among ourselves; we must work as a team." By inviting the participation of union leaders from the very start, Carlzon got them to see the service program as in the best interests of all employees as well as the company. He made sure they had a significant voice in what was happening.

At the Boston Edison Company, a 100-year-old electric utility serving most of Massachusetts, President Stephen Sweeney recently approached union leaders in the same way. The leaders of both the physical workers' union and the clerical and professional workers' union had several significant issues that might have blocked the new total-service-excellence program Sweeney believed was essential to the future of the organization. With the union leaders involved at the outset of the program and with certain major aspects of the plan redirected to meet their concerns, they and the executives agreed at the outset to exempt this crucially important program from the customary adversarial treatment. Union leaders announced their unqualified support of the objectives of the program and played a key role in the employee research involved in launching the effort.

THE MIDDLE MANAGEMENT PROBLEM

As we have moved into the service era and organizations have been looking less and less like manufacturing structures cast in the image of General Motors, the middle management problem has emerged as a more and more troubling one. The classical GM middle management structure—which Frederick Taylor was unable to anticipate early in the century—has brought with it a sense of increasing exasperation on the part of executives and junior managers alike.

Top managers typically feel that middle managers:

Ignore or passively resist new initiatives that come from the executive level.

Don't convey the spirit or the meaning of top management's philosophy and direction to their subordinates.

Don't take initiative and don't provide strong leadership to their organizations.

Cling to rules and regulations in making decisions, rather than proceed on the basis of common sense and the big picture.

Stifle initiative in the lower ranks by squelching new or untried ideas and forcing compliance with traditional ways of doing things.

Some management theorists and frustrated executives have even recommended that we simply eliminate middle managers. "Just get rid of them; we don't need them anyway," the philosophy goes. Some have offered the view that middle managers are merely conduits for information, and that as the computer makes knowledge organizations more effective by speeding up and simplifying the flow of information, middle managers will eventually cease to exist. But this view leaves out some very important realities about life in organizations. Middle management may be more than a mere vestige of GM management. It tends to have a life of its own. Just getting rid of middle managers may not be the simple fix some conceive it to be.

Indeed, the medicine can be more damaging than the disease in some instances. In one hospital, for example, the nursing executive decided nursing directors and head nurses were no longer needed; *all* nurses should work at the bedside. She proceeded to rip out the entire management structure of the nursing organization, dismissing some managers and reassigning others to floor-nurse positions. The result was chaos. The nursing organization was unprepared for the problems of decentralized decision making, resource allocation, and operational communications. Morale took a nosedive and the collective stress level went off the meter. The executives began to realize the middle managers must have been doing something after all.

As management consultant Peter Drucker observes, "Reorganization is major surgery. One doesn't just cut." And just eliminating a whole level of the organization without rethinking roles and relationships is irresponsible as well as dangerous.

Yet it does seem clear that the role and contribution of middle managers in service organizations is due for redefinition. In many organizations, they seem to be limited to the functions of "pointing with pride and viewing with alarm" and little else.

If we don't eliminate middle managers, we will have to find ways to enfranchise them as leaders. They will play an increasingly crucial role as executives try to mobilize their organizations to make service quality the driving idea.

THE FAILURE OF MBO

One of the great unfulfilled promises of the structural-intellectual model of GM management was *management by objectives,* or MBO. Drucker and a number of other early theorists and writers stressed the importance of having objectives for people to work toward. Human beings work more effectively and with greater motivation when they know what they are supposed to accomplish than when they simply follow microscopic instructions and perform therbligs. This view evolved into the idea of MBO as a way to structure work.

MBO seemed to offer a special promise as organizations became more complex and knowledge-intensive. It seemed ideally suited for nonmanufacturing organizations, including even government, in which the product did not automatically structure the work. People in white-collar jobs, especially people in professional jobs like sales, engineering, marketing, and administration, needed aiming points, or objectives, to help them become self-directing. This was the big promise of MBO—it would make the worker self-managing. All we had to do was define for the worker what his or her objectives should be, and we didn't have to worry about day-to-day direction at the task level. We could even have the worker participate in defining the objectives, so he or she would have no trouble accepting them and working toward them with self-generated commitment.

We fell into the same trap with MBO that we fell into with the other management diseases like motivation, productivity, performance appraisal, unionism, and middle management: we kept assuming life is linear and people would act like things. I still believe the central concept of management by objectives is a valid and extremely important one, but we got wrapped up in the structure at the expense of the idea.

The MBO concept is still alive and well, but the failure of the MBO system approach was, in many ways, an indication of the inability of the GM model of management to deal with the increasing richness, diversity, and complexity of knowledge work and nonmanufacturing organizations.

A NEW IMPERATIVE?

If the Taylor/GM paradigm has withstood all of the historical attempts to topple it and has outlived most of the alternatives offered by its intellectual enemies, who is to say it will ever fade out, or that it even should? It has stood the test of time and has served many an organization. Most of the western business world relies on it, and quite profitably.

Yet, we have seen that it brings with it a kind of self-defeating rigidity that works to oppose the injection of the human element into management thinking, except as an enlightened afterthought. The side effects previously enumerated are significant and worrisome. One might ask how much more effective and profitable western corporations might be if they had solved those problems. Doesn't it seem that the typical worker is operating at about half-speed, at least in terms of psychological commitment to performance and belief in the value of what he or she is doing for a living? And doesn't it seem that a small increase in the level of energy and enthusiasm on the part of such a huge number of workers could have a huge effect on productivity and quality, especially in service businesses?

Trying to shame managers into "managing as if people mattered" won't work; they will have to see compelling business reasons for adopting an employee-centered approach to business. The ingredients for this view have been around for a long time. We don't seem to need anything substantially new. We need a recipe that puts them together and a compelling need to do so.

I believe the service revolution may provide the compelling need to manage in a people-centered way, and service management may provide the recipe.

NOTES

[1]See Alfred P. Sloan, *My Years at General Motors* (Garden City, N.Y.: Doubleday, 1963).

[2]Peter F. Drucker, *The Concept of the Corporation* (New York: The John Day Company, 1946).

[3]"Advice from the Dr. Spock of Business," *Business Week,* September 28, 1987.

[4]See Peter Cohen, *The Gospel According to the Harvard Business School* (Garden City, N.Y.: Doubleday, 1963).

[5]Frederick W. Taylor, *The Principles of Scientific Management* (New York: Harper & Brothers, 1911).

[6]"A Ban on Non-Designer Jeans . . .," *San Diego Tribune,* July 20, 1987.

CHAPTER 7

TURNING THE PYRAMID UPSIDE DOWN

A leader is best when people barely know he exists.
Not so good when people obey and acclaim him,
Worst when they despise him.
Fail to honor people,
They fail to honor you.
But of a good leader, who talks little,
When his work is done, his aim fulfilled,
They will all say "We did this ourselves."

—Lao Tzu
The Way of Life

REVISING THE PARADIGM

It doesn't seem feasible, or even necessary, to throw out the GM model of management altogether, but we certainly are due for a revision. Almost all of the counter theories of the last 30 years or so have been trying to accomplish roughly the same thing: loosen up the structural paradigm of western management thought and humanize it. The need is there, the appetite is there, and the imperative is there. We need the makings of a broader paradigm that will retain the advantages of the GM model while it stretches the thinking of managers about how to run organizations that perform rather than produce.

The service management concept may be the basis for that new, broader paradigm. It has shown itself capable, over the past few short years, of captivating the attention of top managers in many kinds of businesses, including some not traditionally thought of as service businesses. It has a way of inviting managers to think original thoughts about their organizations and to start looking at their businesses in different ways.

For the service management paradigm to be successful in displacing the GM model, it will have to provide most of the same benefits the GM model does, as well or better. And it will have to offer extra benefits over and above the GM way of thinking. It will have to answer questions for top executives about strategy, market positioning, and corporate direction. It will have to give managers a way to organize and deploy resources and give them a focus for their attention in supporting the day-to-day work. It will have to give frontline workers a way to think about their jobs in terms of effectiveness and show them what's really important in the day's work. And it will have to provide a framework for thinking about the overall organization and making it work on behalf of the business mission.

Service management seems to offer all these prerequisites in some measure or other. It is a transformational concept that recasts the original thinking process that made the GM paradigm so compelling and brings it out in a new form, without some of the side effects discussed previously. We can contrast the service management model with the GM model in a number of significant ways.

Economic Precept.   The idea behind GM thinking is productivity of capital and labor. Careful control of costs, in a context of parity with competitors with respect to product value, makes the company profitable. In contrast, the idea behind service management thinking is that product quality, i.e., the quality of the service as perceived by the customer, drives profit. In other words, if the quality is there, the profit will follow. Cost structure is still important, but becomes subservient to the trade-offs made on behalf of customer impact.

Work Focus.   In the GM framework, the worker should keep his or her attention on the tasks assigned by the boss; performance of these tasks against preestablished work standards will lead to the ultimate good. In the service management framework, the employee must focus his or her attention on the quality of the customer's experience at the moments of truth; each contact employee becomes the manager of his or her particular moments of truth. There is a shift from an activity orientation to an outcome orientation.

Measurement Criteria. In the GM framework, managers evaluate performance by measuring the output of the frontline workers. Note that they typically do not measure themselves; usually, everyone down through the first-line supervisor is exempt from the normative analysis of their daily work—only the frontline employees get measured. In the service management paradigm, the primary focus of measurement is external; it is the moments of truth that count. Service management recognizes that many things have to happen for the moments of truth to come out well and that the role of the employee is only one component. By focusing attention on the quality of service as perceived by the customers at the various moments of truth, service management considers the whole organization responsible for performance, not just the frontline worker.

Supervisory/Management Focus. The GM model sees the job of the middle manager or frontline supervisor as assuring that workers carry out preestablished job tasks, in compliance with preestablished standards. Their policies, decisions, and interventions should shape employee behavior in the direction of task performance. Service management, in contrast, sees the manager's job, at any level, as resourceful to the frontline employees who have to serve the customers. The mission of managers is to *enable* rather than direct or control, and their decisions and actions should help make the employees more effective managers of the moments of truth.

Organizational Focus. In the GM paradigm, the organization is the message, so to speak. The organizational structure, as a system for deploying resources, becomes the foremost intellectual reality. Structure, process, and legislative control become the primary motifs in the quest for effectiveness. In contrast, the service management paradigm sees organizational structure and apparatus as standing in support of frontline workers, not as exerting control over them. The function of the organization, in this view, is merely to help them make the most valuable impact on their customers. It has no other reason for existing, and when it fails to serve that purpose, it needs changing.

Executive Focus. In the GM perspective, the job of senior management is to preside over the organization and to exert control through structure and process. Service management, in contrast, represents the primary role of senior executives as creating and maintaining a service culture, in which putting the customer first is the principal preoccupation. The key leaders must exert the force of their authority and personalities to advance the primary values of a customer-driven organization.

Figure 7–1 illustrates the contrasts between the GM model of management and the service management paradigm.

TURNING THE PYRAMID UPSIDE DOWN

This paradigm shift from manufacturing management to service management is revolutionary in concept. It is tantamount to turning the traditional pyramid of authority upside down. We have always drawn the organization chart of the typical company with the executives at the top, various subordinate managers in charge of the different boxes on the diagram, and the frontline workers at the bottom, as in Figure 7–2. The geometric implications of this familiar diagram are profound. Putting the employees at the bottom of the heap implies very strongly that they are the least important—or the least influential—participants in the relationship.

Another conceptual flaw in the traditional pyramid diagram of authority is that the customer usually does not appear on the chart. This can be a dangerous oversight because it creates an introverted, organizationally centered conception of reality. In a customer-driven, service-oriented business, the customer should show up somewhere on the diagram.

The service management paradigm suggests that the customer is the *starting point* for defining the business and that we should represent the customer as a key element in the relationships we are trying to describe with the diagram, as shown in Figure 7–3. Because the frontline contact employees are the ones who can make or break the customer's perception of quality at the moment

FIGURE 7–1
Service Management versus GM Management

General Motors Thinking	← Focus →	Service Management Thinking
Productivity of capital and labor drive profit	THE ECONOMIC PRECEPT	Quality of service drives profit
Performance of assigned tasks; meeting job standards	THE WORK FOCUS	Managing moments of truth; assuring customer perceptions of outcome
Normative measures of output	THE MEASUREMENT CRITERIA	Evidence of customer satisfaction
Control and compliance with standards	THE SUPERVISORY/ MANAGEMENT FOCUS	Enablement, support, and assistance
Structure, process, and legislative control	THE ORGANIZATIONAL FOCUS	Support and alignment of resources behind frontline people
Managing through structure	THE EXECUTIVE FOCUS	Creating and maintaining a service culture

of truth, they are the next most important element in the thinking process. Only then do we come to the managers, whose job it is to support and help frontline people in their mission of pleasing the customers.

This upside-down pyramid is a dramatic metaphor for the service-driven organization. The inverted relationships have powerful implications for the way managers relate to employees. The

FIGURE 7–2
Traditional Pyramid Of Authority

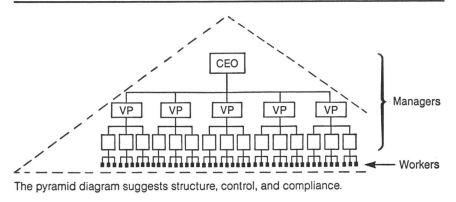

The pyramid diagram suggests structure, control, and compliance.

inversion of priorities and the recasting of the roles of managers do not imply that managers become any less powerful or less in authority. But they do imply that each manager takes on a new role component and a new point of view. Without relinquishing their responsibilities for setting direction, formulating strategy, making decisions, enforcing priorities, and guiding the day-to-day activi-

FIGURE 7–3
Turning the Pyramid of Authority Upside Down

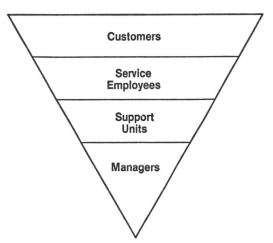

The upside-down pyramid suggests support to the front line.

ties, service-oriented managers must also embrace the roles of supporter, helper, and enabler.

Jan Carlzon of Scandinavian Airlines repeatedly says to his managers at all levels of the organization, "Look, you are not here to dictate to the frontline people. You are here to help them—to support them. And when they come to you for help, you have to listen to them, and not the other way around." Carlzon acknowledges that this can be very difficult for many managers, especially those who rose through the ranks from the front line. But he is absolutely unrelenting in his insistence that managers be resourceful to the frontline people, who are handling the moments of truth.

Carlzon also believes frontline people should have much more autonomy and authority to act than traditional management gives them. He refers to the process of flattening the pyramid by reducing the effect of the decision-making layers of the organization and creating more freedom at the front line.

Turning the pyramid upside down will be a tall order for many organizations, especially in view of the dominant influence of the traditional authority concepts inherent in the Taylor/GM management model. But there is clear evidence that more and more service businesses are attempting to do just that. It will be very interesting and enlightening to see how they go about it, what works, what doesn't, and whether the concept turns out to have long-range validity and acceptance for the broad mainstream of western managers.

Those readers who are aficionados of the left brain/right brain theory of human thinking will recognize that Figures 7–1 through 7–3 convey a transition from a left-brained conception of management to a right-brained conception. The service management conception is more nonlinear, holistic, global, human oriented, intuitive, and less analytically structured than the GM approach, which is more linear, structural, elemental, analytical, and normative.

The trouble with theories like the one presented above is that they are easy and fun to conceive of and think about, but they are the devil to bring into reality in the rough-and-tumble world of everyday business. But that is the challenge facing managers today. To capitalize on the possibilities of service management, they will have to loosen up the old GM paradigm, humanize it, make it much more flexible, and shift the focus of attention from the internals of the organization to the customer interface and to the working people who are responsible for giving quality to that interface.

Managers will have to learn to live with a greater degree of employee autonomy, which implies a higher level of ambiguity for them as leaders. They will have to give up some of their reliance on the generic, rule-based solution and be willing to tailor their leadership more to the variations in circumstances at the front line. And they will have to shift their attention from controlling to supporting. This will require a self-conscious process of deliberately assessing and rethinking what goes on in the organization.

One organization that is consciously attempting to turn the pyramid upside down is Toronto Dominion Bank, one of Canada's largest. Part of the creativity that characterizes the executive approach is exemplified in the way top management organized the company's annual management conference. In anticipation of my keynote speech to the managers, which was to be titled "Turning the Pyramid Upside Down," executives ordered a novelty-products firm to make 200 miniature pyramids of polished mahogany. They sent a pyramid to each of the managers in advance of the conference with a personal letter from President Robin Korthals asking them to think about two questions before they arrived in Toronto for the conference:

1. What does this pyramid have to do with customer service?
2. How can you make it stand on its tip?

After my speech, the managers worked in small break-out groups to answer Korthals' two questions. During those sessions, each manager received the second piece to the puzzle: a matching wood base for the pyramid. The base had a depression cut into it to accept the tip of the pyramid and hold it in position. Using various creative problem-solving techniques, they explored the associations and implications of the metaphor of turning the pyramid upside down and supporting it in its new configuration.

PUTTING THE CUSTOMER FIRST

Colin Marshall, chief executive officer of British Airways, speaks of putting the customer first.

We are in the service business, and our objective is to be the world's leading airline in service quality. That means putting the customer first in all we do.

"Putting the customer first" has the makings of a great slogan—a glittering platitude—it is short, snappy, and phonetically pleasing. But how can we make it into something more than a slogan? How can we make it a reality?

It is one thing for executives to toss the slogan about and to talk glowingly about how the customer is king; it is quite another thing for them to make major decisions and resource commitments in that spirit.

What are the hallmarks of the company that puts its customers first? How do we know one when we see it? For starters, we can agree that truly customer-first companies:

1. Think and talk about their customers a lot.
2. Keep assessing their customers' perceptions.
3. Tend to resolve priority issues in favor of the most profitable impact on the customer.
4. Give in, compromise, or add value for the customer in dispute situations where the value of goodwill exceeds the economic stake.
5. Recover conscientiously from blunders or mishandled moments of truth; make amends to the customer who has received poor treatment.
6. Employ a "whatever it takes" policy in trying to remedy the situation for a dissatisfied customer or one with a special need.
7. Redesign systems, redeploy resources, and turn sacred cows out to pasture when they get in the way of service quality.

This last point can be a real test. When it comes to major decisions about resources, many executives flinch. "We really didn't mean it *that* way," they say. "Let's not go to extremes." One of Jan Carlzon's first major decisions as head of Scandinavian Airlines involved such a test. When Carlzon studied the impact of SAS's new fuel-efficient high-passenger-load Airbuses, he concluded they were not helping SAS operate in a customer-first way.

The company had just spent $120 million for four of the aircraft and had options for another eight. The original idea behind the Airbus was to make the main air routes between Copenhagen's Kastrup airport and the major airports of the European continent highly profitable by maximizing passenger loads with fuel-efficient equipment.

The problem, Carlzon realized, was that SAS was trying to force its customers to accept inconvenient flights by routing them through Copenhagen and loading them onto the Airbuses instead of having direct flights from the various Scandinavian cities to their destinations. It was great for economics but not great for service. Carlzon theorized that SAS would gradually lose market share to other airlines like Lufthansa and Swissair, which operated nonstop and direct flights.

As a result, Carlzon decided to mothball the Airbuses and change the route structure to make it more competitive, with nonstop and direct flights using DC–9 aircraft more suited to the smaller passenger loads. His decision was a clear case of putting the money where the mouth is. It was a very costly decision in the short run, and one that horrified many onlookers. But Carlzon believed that the customer-first avenue made more sense in the long run. Judging by SAS's market performance, one could argue that he made a successful bet.

EMOTIONAL LABOR: A NEW REALIZATION

Industrial psychologists and management theorists are beginning to recognize a distinctly modern aspect of work, especially in service businesses: *emotional labor*. It has been around for a long time, but we are just now starting to understand it as a different kind of work from manufacturing work. Emotional labor is any kind of work in which the employee's feelings are the tools of his or her trade. That is, his or her psychological, emotional, creature reactions get involved as a consequence of some aspect of the job itself. *Feeling* is in some way a part of job performance.

Examples of jobs that involve extreme degrees of emotional labor include psychiatrist, social worker, doctor, nurse, paramedic, firefighter, and police officer. These people have to deal directly with other human beings on a regular basis and often with people who are in distress. It is very difficult to do these kinds of work without having the feelings of the afflicted people rub off on the person doing the work. After all, the patient in therapy has to deal with only one distraught, maladjusted person—him- or her-self—while the psychiatrist has to deal with a number of them during any working day.

Service jobs, and in particular public-contact jobs, can involve a relatively high degree of emotional labor. A person who handles lost-baggage claims all day for an airline, for example, deals with a lot of disturbed people. Few of them are happy, and seldom does a traveller stop by the lost luggage counter to wish the person behind it a pleasant day.

Jobs involving low levels of emotional labor include manual or construction worker, accountant, engineer, computer operator, graphic artist, and writer. These jobs usually involve relatively minimal human contact and relatively little conflict or negative feelings. An accountant can become distressed over the implications of a column of figures or have to deal with someone else who is distressed about them, but this is not the sum and substance of the job itself.

Almost all jobs involve some human demand in terms of emotional labor, and some days even the most benign of activities can turn into a stressful experience. But most jobs fall somewhere in the middle of the scale of emotional labor, between high intensity and low intensity.

Jobs like waiter or waitress, restaurant host or hostess, counter clerk, grocery checker, flight attendant, and telephone operator all have a fairly heavy dose of emotional labor.

Even customer-contact jobs that go along positively involve emotional labor. Merely interacting with another human being, even over the telephone, induces a certain normal amount of stress. The person handling the situation must be fully alert, concentrating on the matter at hand, and conscious of doing the best possible job for the customer.

Psychologists have identified a distinctive reaction in human beings called the *contact-overload syndrome*. It befalls people whose jobs put them in one-to-one contact with many, many people on a constant, repeated basis. Think about a person who processes driver's license applications all day, or rings up meals for hundreds of people at the cashier position in a busy cafeteria, or processes hundreds of telephone stock transactions each day. Having to interact with one stranger after another, over and over, all day, causes a kind of emotional fatigue reaction to set in. A person can handle just so many of these miniature emotional events in a given period before he or she begins to feel tense, overloaded, tired, and jaded. How many times have you heard a service worker say, "I just can't bear to look at another customer today"?

It appears that some people can tolerate high-frequency contact much more than others. Some people just find it too uncomfortable and psychically draining to deal with a steady flow of strangers for hours on end. In other words, people vary in their ability to handle emotional labor. Many managers have not fully appreciated this fact; indeed, most of our management theory has overlooked it.

Contact overload and the other side effects of stressful emotional labor can show up in the working person's feelings, attitudes, and behavior in several significant ways:

> Feelings of apathy, lassitude, psychological withdrawal, alienation from the immediate situation, and hostility toward the people who are the source of the overload, i.e., the customers.
>
> Physical fatigue, tension, elevated stress levels, moodiness, and irritability.
>
> Indifference toward the job and the customer; a don't-give-a-damn demeanor that puts the customer off; loss of interest in the quality of one's work; lack of personal pride or sense of achievement.
>
> Detachment of one's feelings from the situation; a "flat-affect" emotional reaction pattern that becomes robotic and programmed.

This reaction to emotional labor can have two serious consequences. First, it is unhealthy for the person having it. It can induce psychological stress that can carry over into his or her personal life as well as make work life unpleasant and unrewarding.

Second, the negative emotional reaction experienced by the employee spills over onto the customer, contaminating the quality of the moments of truth. An employee who is apathetic, withdrawn, emotionally flat or hostile, and disinterested in his or her job will transfer those feelings to the customer and create a negative impression of him- or herself and the company.

This simple concept of emotional labor explains why all of us, as customers, see so much toxic behavior on the part of frontline service employees who are supposed to be giving us good service. The person we're tempted to describe as lazy, indifferent, uncaring, and not qualified for a service job may actually be in the advanced stages of burnout because of contact overload. In other words, a great deal of negative behavior on the part of frontline service people is *normal behavior*. That doesn't mean we have to approve of it or consider it acceptable, but it does mean we need to understand it and deal with it in human and humane terms.

A prior chapter discusses the Seven Sins of Service, a number of which stem from the psychological problems of employees who are having trouble coping with the demands of emotional labor. These are the things organizations and workers do to customers that damage their perceptions of quality of service.

The GM concept of management doesn't have a provision for assessing the psychological impact of the job on the person. The assumption is usually that, if the person can't handle the job, he or she must be incompetent in some way and we should get somebody else. A more enlightened view suggests that rethinking the structure of the job, rethinking the rationales for assigning people to jobs, and making provisions for helping people cope better with emotional labor can make service work more effective as well as more healthy for human beings.

The problem of emotional labor is one we are going to have to understand better and deal with explicitly in job design, employee selection, and employee training. We need to look at the ways in which we have productionized many of our service jobs—in the best style of Frederick Taylor and GM management—and find ways to relieve some of the contact stress that employees experience. We need to learn more about identifying people who are more resilient to the demands of emotional labor and help those who are less resilient find work more suited to their orientation. And we need to invest much more in the training of contact workers, to help them maintain high levels of energy and positive feelings throughout the day.

LESS "MANAGEMENT," MORE LEADERSHIP

One of the legacies of the GM paradigm of organizations and the management thereof is that:

Today's employee is overmanaged and underled.

More and more management theorists are recognizing it, commenting about it, and writing about it. More and more executives are sensing that the people in their organizations need something different from them than the traditional management they have been providing for so many years. I have talked with quite a few executives who, at the point of launching service programs, have looked at their organizations and discerned a need for a stronger, more vibrant internal culture. They have begun asking themselves, "How can we as executives provide the kind of values, direction, motivation, and energy our people need to help them tackle this new mission?"

A consequence of many years of application of the GM model is that "management" in many organizations has degenerated to nothing more than "administration." This is especially true in large, stable companies operating in mature industries, like restaurant chains, utilities, banks and other financial institutions, and hospitals. It is especially true in government agencies, educational institutions, and other large nonprofit organizations.

Ideally, what we call management should be a complete constellation of skills, including original thinking and application of human values, not merely slavish adherence to structure and procedure. People need more from their managers than just rules, regulations, policies, procedures, and directives. They need leadership as well as administration.

An appropriately broad concept of management, as a set of skills, includes a reasonable balance of the personal and the impersonal; the social and the technical; the intuitive and the rational. The effective manager must have vision and perspective; be willing and able to establish strategy and direction and stick to them; exert personal influence, i.e., the skillful use of self; project and advocate important values; get involved with the people as helper, supporter, guide, and colleague; communicate clearly and strongly to influence people toward the chosen direction; develop people and demand the best from them; and make sure the feedback and rewards they get are making it worthwhile for them to work enthusiastically in support of the business mission.

Doing business in a service environment ups the ante significantly on managers at all levels. It requires that senior executives serve as the flag carriers for the service mission and play their full roles as builders and enhancers of the service culture. It requires that middle managers step up to their necessary roles as leaders and advocates, rather than functionaries and interpreters of rules. And it requires that junior managers—the tactical-level supervisors—fully accept and act within their roles as leaders and supporters to the frontline service people. This, we can hope, will be one of the great legacies of the service management concept.

THE EMPLOYEES AS YOUR FIRST "MARKET"

If your employees are not sold on the quality of the service your organization provides and on the importance of their roles in providing it, they will never sell your customers on it. We will have to start thinking of the employees as a "market" in a sense. By this I mean that we will have to literally *sell* the idea of service quality to them. In many cases it will be an easy sell; in some cases it will be a very difficult one. We need to make sure they believe in the idea of putting the customer first, and that they take seriously the organization's efforts to do so.

For a major service program to succeed in your organization, a necessary first step is to win the commitment of the people who ultimately control its success: the frontline working people. Commitment requires that they:

1. Understand the objective and the need for achieving it.
2. Believe in the program and feel it is worthwhile.
3. Believe it has the possibility of succeeding.
4. Feel it will be personally worthwhile for them.

These criteria suggest what you must do to win their commitment.

First, you must conceptualize the program's objective clearly and simply. You must have a compelling reason to undertake it and a compelling explanation of that reason. You must be able to dramatize the value of the effort in human terms. And you must be able to explain it to everyone, every day, in simple and compelling language.

Second, you must be able to show clearly how the program will appeal to the customer, and consequently how it will benefit the organization. You need more than platitudes at this point. You need demonstrable evidence of the impact service quality has on the customer's choices about where he or she does business or about how he or she is willing to spend money. You need to have your homework together for your own sense of conviction as well as to support the convictions of the frontline people.

You need a program plan and an overall philosophy of implementation that can make sense to the rank-and-file working people. You need to have credibility with them, so that when you publicize your program and your plan, they will be willing to embrace it as making sense. Your plan has to show evidence of unwavering top management support and the willingness to invest the necessary resources to make it work. If you go to them with nothing but a batch of platitudes, slogans, and pep talks, while the plan shows that you really don't intend to make an investment in service quality, they will smoke you out. They know when top management is serious and when it's not.

And finally, the whole undertaking must proceed in the spirit of cooperation, support to the frontline people, and teamwork all across the organization. The objective must carry with it the possibility that the mission of achieving it will be personally rewarding. It does not necessarily have to be a promise of more money, although that is one of the most appealing payoffs. People have to genuinely believe the program is being undertaken with their support and commitment, not by trying to drive them into it. There needs to be some element of pride in the company and a sense of meaning in taking on the challenge.

You probably face a bigger selling job with your managers than with your employees, particularly with your middle managers. Frontline supervisors typically respond to the same kinds of appeals as the workers, because they share many of the same experiences and views as a result of their tactical orientation to the

work itself. Typically, however, middle managers have trouble figuring out how to participate energetically in top-down programs of
the type required to launch a major service-quality commitment.

Often, top management gives the go-ahead to a big new service
venture on the assumption that the middle managers understand
it, believe in it, and are as excited about it as the chiefs are. In
reality, they may just be smiling and "shining you on," giving the
impression that they are "on board." Thereafter, they may do little
or nothing to drive the program forward. They probably will not
do anything consciously to impede the program, but neither will
they lend their energy, enthusiasm, or creativity to it. They may
become what middle managers are often perceived to be: an inertial blob of Jello in the middle of the organization, neither helping
nor hurting, but just sitting on the bench.

Middle management inertia is by no means universal. In some
organizations, the middle managers grab the ball and exert very
strong leadership in support of what they believe in. In other organizations, there may be general inertia at the middle levels, but
there still may be individual managers who are highly proactive
and visionary in their leadership. But in general, given the historical image of middle managers as inertial bureaucrats, it makes
sense to test very carefully to see what kind of commitment is
there, which managers really have it, and what kinds of personal
skills they have for making a service program successful.

This early process of commitment building can be crucially
important. Without energy and commitment, the organization itself becomes its own worst enemy. With it, most of the obstacles
and pitfalls eventually give way to the energy and drive that lie
behind the commitment.

THE SHARED-FATE CONCEPT

Some time ago I listened to an interview with a noted Japanese
executive, "Mike" Morita, then head of Sony Corporation's
Rancho Bernardo manufacturing facility in California. Asked to
explain his view of the differences between Japanese management
and American management, Morita described it this way:

In the Japanese business culture, we think of our jobs in terms of *shared fate*. That means that all employees in the company share the same fate. The success—or failure—of the company affects all of us the same. The only way we can make our lives secure as individuals is to make sure the company remains competitive. We have to work together to make the best products we possibly can. So it is extremely important that each person understands the needs of the company, and each is willing to contribute his or her best efforts to make it successful. This is the important aspect of the Japanese way: that each person's contribution goes together with the contribution of every other person for the best result.

Morita's statement holds a profoundly important lesson for American managers. Notwithstanding the fact that we have been bombarded and browbeaten with Japanese management over the past five years or so, we had better listen carefully to ideas like this. Clearly, we cannot import the Japanese culture into the United States. We cannot transplant the Japanese cultural substrate into the American business organization, nor would we want to if we could. But we can capitalize on the possibilities inherent in certain Japanese attitudes and make those attitudes work for us in our cultural reality.

In a service business, or any business, all of the people in the organization do share the same fate, whether they believe they do or not. You may choose not to believe in the law of gravity, but that does not exempt you from its influence. In the same way, the law of shared fate applies whether you like it or not. If the front end of the ship goes down, the back end is going to go down with it. Blaming and finger-pointing are irrelevant when the thing is sinking.

One reason the shared fate ethic is not more widespread in American business is probably the rugged individualist theme that runs through so much of American culture. The Japanese have no real counterpart to our "make it on your own" value. Many Americans take a fierce pride in standing out from the crowd, in going against the popular trend. But to most Japanese, belonging is more important than almost any other life value, including sometimes life itself. Disapproval, rejection, or ostracism by one's family, social group, or work group is one of the most distressing experiences possible for most Japanese. In most cases, acceptance and approval by the work group has as much impact on a person's behavior and needs to belong as it does for his or her immediate family. Many Japanese simply cannot survive psychically—or believe they cannot—without the acceptance and approval of the social group to which they belong.

For the Japanese, the shared fate ethic comes with the territory. They didn't necessarily cultivate and develop it; they simply found it necessary for their society to function. But the case is considerably different for Americans. Working together, helping one another, cooperating and compromising, and team work are only circumstantially valuable to most Americans. That is, they can accept those themes when they seem evidently useful to them as individuals. At other times, other values can override them.

The lack of a shared fate ethic in western countries tends to aggravate union-management relationships, for example. It is more typical for a worker to identify with his or her own work force or with the union in the face of a "we-they" standoff with management than it is to identify with the overall idea of the company. This can create a sinking ship situation in which the union and the executives are fighting bitterly while the whole company goes down the tubes as a result of the conflict. More than one American company has closed its doors because executives and union leaders could not find a common ground of shared values and shared benefits.

Some years ago, I got a significant insight into Japanese labor politics during a visit to a company in Nagoya. The head of marketing in a custom textile firm invited me to visit the plant for a tour and a chat with the executive team. We had an interesting discussion over tea and went for a walk around the facility. I asked my host, "Shiggie, (his nickname) are your employees unionized?" "Yes," he said. "Almost all of them are in the union." When I asked about the union-management relationship, he smiled and said, "It's not a problem. Every year they have a strike. We give them a raise and they go back to work."

I was taken by the matter-of-fact way in which he described the relationship. It was as if the strike were a ceremonial reminder to management that the employees had rights and clout. Nobody mistook it for a major conflict. It was part of the relationship. Each side recognized that it needed the other; for them the strike was simply a matter of role clarification.

Certainly not all Japanese firms have such benign labor politics, by any means. But the Japanese culture does seem to offer a context for greater labor peace than that of many western countries, especially those like Australia.

The shared fate ethic must be alive and reasonably well for a service-quality effort to succeed in a business organization, whatever its size. Some organizations have it and cherish it; others are a long way from it. Probably most are somewhere in the middle, i.e., it may be alive but not feeling well. In many cases, careful attention by senior management to developing the shared fate atmosphere is one of the important first items of business.

Some indications that a shared fate feeling is prevalent in the organization are:

1. The employees have a high level of personal respect for the top executives; they trust them and put stock in their word; they feel confident that someone is at the helm and there is a clear direction.
2. They consider the organization basically a good place to work; they personally identify with the company.
3. They feel a sense of mission, a desire to be part of a big undertaking.
4. They observe their managers modeling cooperative and collaborative behavior in dealing with one another.
5. They typically pitch in to help one another; they share information, fill in for one another, and take the trouble to keep one another up to date on important news.

Like other organizational values, shared fate does not come about by executive fiat. It is, however, a state of affairs that top management can bring about by doing the right things. When the chief executive and his or her team have established a clear direction and strategy, work together effectively as a team, speak with a common voice and a common set of values, expect and get team work and cooperation among their subordinate managers, and show genuine care and concern for the well-being of the frontline employees, all the necessary components are in place for a shared fate philosophy of working together. In such a case, it is much easier for the service program to generate the interest, enthusiasm, and employee commitment that will make it succeed.

MANAGEMENT ITSELF BECOMES A SERVICE

At the risk of seeming to carry the service management concept to the point of making it a theology, I suggest that, in a service culture, the practice of management becomes a service. Without giving up their responsibilities for setting direction, allocating resources, establishing priorities, making decisions, and guiding the work, managers must broaden their concepts of their roles to include supporting and enabling the frontline workers in their handling of the moments of truth.

This precept applies equally to the chief executive and to the lowest-ranking member of the management family. Here is an example.

One afternoon in 1982, Jan Carlzon, president of the Scandinavian Airlines System, telephoned one of his pilots. Carlzon had noticed, by consulting the video monitor installed in his office, that the pilot's flight had taken off late. Because Carlzon had decreed that on-time takeoff was to be one of the basic driving ideas of SAS's service image, he took a special interest in punctuality. But rather than berate the pilot, Carlzon gently reminded him of the importance he attached to on-time departure and asked, "What can we in management be doing to help you get off the ground on time? Are there problems beyond your control that we should be trying to solve? Do you need assistance that you don't have? How can we make it easier for you to meet the objective?"

The idea of management as a service comes naturally to many managers, although they might not phrase it in that way. For others, it may offer a new and exciting clarification of their roles as leaders. And for others, it might seem like so much baloney. Some traditionally schooled managers have trouble with "all this touchy-feely crap," as one manager I know calls it. Sadly, many older managers see this "soft-side" view of leadership as an intellectual aberration, although they offer no alternative in the face of the classical problems of employee alienation, demotivation, and disaffection. You as a manager must make your own determination about the idea of management as a service and how you can best work with the people in your organization to achieve high quality service.

If you find the idea of management as a service appealing and potentially practical, here are some things you can do to begin applying it:

1. Regularly ask each of the people you supervise, "What can I do to help you do your job better? What problems do you have that I can help you solve? What's getting in the way of your doing the best job you possibly can?"

2. Think of things that might contribute to their effectiveness; identify possible innovations—improvements in your computer systems, streamlining of procedures, or changing relationships among jobs or units to help them collaborate better.

3. Have regular meetings with the people in your group to review the effectiveness of the whole operation; ask them to identify any organizational procedures, processes, or systems they believe need rethinking or elimination; make cooperation and mutual effectiveness a regular matter of discussion and analysis.

4. Stop wasting their time with directives and demands that have no other purpose but to feed your management neuroses; review every policy, procedure, rule, or regulation you have ever established from the point of view of its contribution to the effectiveness of the people doing the work; eliminate every report you can do without; overcome your anxieties about being in charge, and let them get back to work; you'll know when they need you. Think less about the management of service and more about the service of management.

PUTTING THE EMPLOYEES IN CHARGE

One of the elements of the service management paradigm that offers the most promise, but which will probably be most misunderstood, is the philosophy of putting the frontline employees in charge. Carlzon of SAS tells a very revealing story about an episode in his organization:

> I came into one of our airports one early morning, and I noticed that the information system had broken down—the information system which told you where the baggage from your flight was coming. There were queues of people in the arrival hall. I was really angry, because it was so easy to solve. Somebody could just put up a handwritten sign to tell you where your luggage was coming in.
>
> So I went to the girl at the counter and I said, "For heaven's sake, why can't you make it by your hand—a sign—just to tell people?"
>
> "That's exactly what I think," she said. "So I went to my manager and asked him for permission to put up a sign. But my manager said, 'Well, but it's no use; the data system will be in order again in a couple of hours, so it's no problem.'"
>
> "When was this?" I asked. "It was one week ago," she said.

This was one of many cases in Carlzon's experience—and SAS is no different from other organizations—where the frontline employee had a better grasp of the fundamentals of the situation than the manager did. Incidents like this one began to have a profound effect on Carlzon's thinking. He began to form the conclusion that authority in SAS was misallocated and that frontline people were capable of handling much more responsibility than traditional management thinking allowed. He began to shift the SAS culture in the direction of empowering the frontline people to make more decisions and to solve problems on their own, without consulting their managers.

Carlzon's philosophy of putting the frontline people in charge caused a great deal of discomfort for his managers, especially middle managers. Carlzon refused to endorse their actions just because they were part of the in-group—the management family. He insisted that their actions make sense in the context of a customer-driven culture, and he was just as likely to agree with the actions of the employee when disputes arose, if the employee had acted in a customer-first manner.

In his book *Moments of Truth,* Carlzon tells of an episode in which an employee outflanked a department manager in serving the customers.[1]

> One day an SAS flight across Sweden had fallen far behind schedule because of snow. Taking responsibility for the situation, the purser decided on her own to compensate the customers for their inconvenience by offering free coffee and biscuits (cookies). She

knew from experience that, because she was offering them at no charge, she would need about 40 additional servings. So she went to catering and ordered the extra coffee and biscuits.

The SAS catering supervisor turned her down. It was against regulations to request more than the amount of food allotted to a particular flight, and the supervisor refused to budge. But the purser wasn't thwarted. She noticed a Finnair plane docked at the next gate. Finnair is an external customer of the SAS catering department, and as such is not subject to SAS internal regulations.

Thinking quickly, the SAS purser turned to her colleague in the Finnair plane and asked him to order 40 cups of coffee and 40 biscuits. He placed the order which, according to regulations, the catering supervisor was obligated to fulfill. Then the SAS purser bought the snacks from Finnair with petty cash and served the grateful passengers.

When Carlzon heard of the incident, his reaction was unequivocal: "I think she did exactly the right thing." His view was that, in the new SAS, the only thing that counted was a satisfied customer, and the purser understood and advocated the SAS philosophy better than the supervisor did.

Unfortunately, incidents of this kind can create hard feelings among managers while they are instilling confidence and a sense of autonomy in frontline people. Of the manager's reaction to the incident, Carlzon noted:

> In this case, the purser dared to find a way to circumvent regulations in order to meet the customers' needs—something she surely never would have tried under the old system. At the same time, however, the catering supervisor couldn't understand why a lowly purser had the right to make decisions that had always been in his purview and so he became confused and angry.
>
> Much of the fault for this was ours (upper management's). We had let our middle managers down. We had given the front line the right to accept responsibility, yet we hadn't given middle managers viable alternatives to their old role as rule interpreters. We hadn't told middle managers how to handle what might, at first glance, look like a demotion.

The service management philosophy suggests the employees are really the keepers and managers of the moments of truth. Executives who believe in the capacity of frontline people to make good judgments, within a framework of common sense, are changing their thinking about them. Dick Scott, chief operating officer of Longs Drug Stores, a chain of 250 stores in the western United States, told me of this experience in helping store managers rethink the roles of frontline workers in Longs' stores:

> I was standing in one of our stores one day, just watching the goings-on. A number of times I noticed the store manager approving customers' checks brought to him by the cashiers. I watched the process for a while. What happened most of the time was this: the store manager would be talking to somebody about some particular matter, and the checker would stop the line, take the customer's check over to him and stand there while he approved it. The rest of the customers would have to wait for this process every time someone paid by check.
>
> The thing that caught my attention was that the manager didn't really examine the check; he just scribbled his initials on it and handed it back to the clerk. He didn't look over to see what the customer looked like or anything. Most of the time he didn't even interrupt the conversation he was having.
>
> Later on I had a discussion with the manager about approving checks. I suggested that maybe we ought to just let the cashiers approve checks so we could get the customers on their way faster and not hold them up every time. He was horrified at that. He assured me we would end up with a bad check problem that wouldn't quit.
>
> But I said to him, "Let me ask you a question. When she brought you the check for your approval, what thought process went through your mind as you approved it?" He said, "Well, no thought process, really. I didn't give it much thought, to tell the truth."
>
> I said, "That's exactly my point. If you didn't have any thought process going on in *your* head, don't you think we could teach her not to have any thought process go on in *her* head? Don't you think we could teach her to scribble something on the check and get the customer on his way?"

Dick Scott's observation led to the company policy of putting the checkers completely in charge of approving checks. The bad check rate stayed the same as it had been, and the customers felt better about being trusted and treated as if their time was valuable. Approving checks might seem like a small matter, but the change in policy carried an important message to the frontline people. In

Scott's words, "Your job is to satisfy your customers—whatever it takes."

This idea of putting frontline people in charge intrigues many top executives. It also has scary overtones. It is a break with past practice, and we have no experience against which to evaluate it. It apparently caused an enormous uproar in Carlzon's organization, and it is my impression that the middle management wounds have yet to heal because of it.

Put yourself in the place of the middle manager who lost the skirmish with the purser who bought the snacks. The manager is justified in saying to senior management, "Listen, who do you want to be in charge around here? Why do you put people in management jobs and give them policies to follow, if you're going to let every Tom, Dick, and Harry do whatever he damn well pleases? How do you expect me to manage a department if my word doesn't carry any authority?"

It's a tough question, and one that demands a great deal of thought. The higher principle, of course, is doing whatever it takes to make a hit with the customer. Carlzon had said as much, many times, to everyone in the organization, including the manager. The manager had heard the gospel just as the purser had heard it. Yet he chose to stand by the rules when she asked him to bend them. The issue becomes one of common sense and good judgment, not one of authority and entitlement.

Dick Scott of Longs Drug Stores encountered the same reaction from many of his managers when he began to talk to frontline people about doing whatever it takes to satisfy the customer. Some managers would say, "Suppose the customer says, 'OK, to satisfy me, please give me all of the cash in your cash register.' What should the checker do—empty out the cash drawer and give it to the customer?" Scott replied, "Of course not. And I don't think we have any employees working for us who would think that was appropriate. The key is to ask yourself what would be reasonable and appropriate under the circumstances. If that means bending the rules a bit without breaking the company, then that's what I want the employee to do; and you and I don't even need to know about it."

Those who get cold chills at the idea of the frontline employee making judgments and deciding unilaterally what to do for the customer may be thinking too narrowly about risk and payoff. Suppose, for example, upper management had decided the SAS purser made a mistake; she shouldn't have purchased the snacks and given them to the passengers. How much of the company's money would she have wasted? Perhaps $100 or so. When you evaluate the maximum possible financial risk in the situation against the possible payoff in customer satisfaction, you can make a pretty clear case for giving the purser the freedom to act. On any given day, a typical middle manager probably wastes more money than that without even knowing it.

If it were a matter of thousands of dollars, it would have been different. And probably the purser would have acted accordingly. Isn't it reasonable to assume she would have weighed the pros and cons more cautiously and probably would not have made the commitment?

Unfortunately, many managers can't recognize the difference between a hundred-dollar issue and a thousand-dollar issue. They apply the same risk-aversive decision policies to the small and the large issues alike. And even if they could, many of them would still try to overcontrol the distinction by establishing a formal cutoff point on cost, so the employee had discretion up to some level but not above. They would end up at the same place, with the employee boxed in by normative controls. Some people just don't like the idea of taking things as they come and deciding individual issues on their own merits. They like to have everything staked out in advance, and if an issue comes up they weren't prepared for, they take the lowest-risk way out, regardless of the impact on the customer.

It makes good sense to do a wholesale review of the rules and regulations surrounding the frontline employees, both direct-contact employees and support employees. Look at the rule-making and policy-making process *in toto* and find out what it is saying to the worker. Identify rules and procedures that have little real value but hem the worker in and prevent him or her from really responding to the customer. You may be amazed at how little you've been allowing frontline employees to do, and how much they really can do if you place your trust in them.

When you loosen the rules and controls, you may find your employees giving more of themselves to the customer. Many of the most fabulous service stories may be going on right in your organization, right now. Sheraton Corporation's senior vice president for marketing, Bob Collier, likes to brag about a Sheraton desk clerk who went a good deal more than the extra mile for a customer.

According to the story, a distraught guest came to the counter early one morning asking for help with a personal problem. He had to go to an important job interview that morning and had just discovered he had forgotten to bring his dress shoes. The only shoes he had were the jogging shoes he had worn with his jeans on the trip from home. "Do you know of any shoe stores near here?" he asked. "Can I rent some shoes somewhere?"

The Sheraton clerk, noting that he was about the same size as the guest, asked, "What size shoes do you wear?" Learning that he and the guest had feet of approximately the same size, the desk clerk exchanged shoes with the guest. The guest went to the interview wearing the clerk's shoes and the clerk wore the jogging shoes that day.

These are the stories that touch the heart and make a chief executive proud of the people in the company. And they happen when the employees feel empowered and encouraged to do what's right. They invest themselves because they believe in it, not because somebody is telling them to do it.

BUILDING THE SERVICE CULTURE

We have firmly established the precept that, without a service culture in your organization, you can never hope to sustain a long-term commitment to service quality. The only hope of making service a permanent part of the frontline reality is to make it a permanent part of the atmosphere of the company.

I have been using the term culture quite freely in the preceding discussion, and now we need to clarify the idea of culture. What is a culture, where do you get one, and how does it come to be what it is? In my recent book *The Creative Corporation*,[2] I defined *culture* as:

A social context that influences the way people behave and relate.

In the sense of this definition, a *service culture* is one that influences people to behave and relate in service-oriented ways, or in customer-first ways. This means that the signals that influence behavior are heavily colored with the motif of service. The authority figures, the prevailing values, the norms for behaving, and the system of rewards and sanctions all line up to influence people in the direction of high-quality outcomes at the moments of truth.

When your role as a customer puts you into contact with an organization that has a strong service culture, you know it immediately. And if you have a chance to experience the inside of the organization as I frequently have, you can immediately sense the signal system that keeps it oriented to service.

In the Marriott culture, for example, there is an instinctive and automatic impulse to turn toward the customer in thinking about how to run the organization, rather than turn toward the internal structures and processes. Chairman J. Willard "Bill" Marriott, Jr., is constant in his preaching, teaching, and reminding people about the customer and about service.

Marriott is a believer in *visible management*. He flies more than 200,000 miles a year visiting all of the operational locations of the corporation, carrying the message to his managers and to the frontline people. He is famous in the company for dropping into a hotel and quietly chatting with every employee on the property. He puts himself in contact with the lowliest employee just as with the most powerful manager. This style of personal influence has become so well known to his employees that his mere presence on the scene is an automatic reminder to people to check their thinking processes and make sure they are still operating on the service-quality wavelength.

The Disney culture is an interesting case as well. The service culture that prevails at a Disney property such as Disneyland in California or Disney World in Florida is the culture of show business. The Disney style is one of high-value customer service within a context of fantasy. There is an unrelenting attention to cleanliness and eye appeal about all aspects of the park. The workers are clean, tidy, wholesome middle-America kids, trained for polite and helpful dealings with the customers.

Because Disney has created a high-value service product—i.e., fun and fantasy—and backed it with a strong service culture that guarantees a high-quality delivery of the product, it can charge premium prices for admission to the park. People may remark at the prices posted at the entrance to the park, but it would be virtually unthinkable for a family to visit southern California or Florida for the first time and pass up Disneyland because of the price of admission. Disney is preeminent among theme park operators and enjoys the profit advantages that a quality product bestows.

Another outstanding example of a service culture, although less well known, is the Nordstrom department store chain, based in Seattle. The Nordstrom family founded the business on the premise of selling high-quality merchandise—at premium prices—in an atmosphere of intensely personal service to the customers. Nordstrom salespeople try to form long-term relationships with individual customers and develop their business by personal followups and an unusual amount of personal catering.

The business culture allows and encourages the salesperson to take a great deal of initiative in developing the customer relationship. For example, he or she is not confined by the boundaries of the home department as a selling territory. The salesperson can accompany the customer anywhere in the store, helping to locate shirts, ties, shoes, accessories, jewelry, and the like.

Nordstrom is one of those strong-culture companies that have relatively few rules and regulations, relying on the leadership of the store managers and department heads to instill the primary values of service-oriented selling into all new employees. A telling example of the simple way in which Nordstrom management communicates key values to the workers is the fact that the Nordstrom "employee handbook" is a single card, half the size of a standard sheet of paper. One side of it has nothing more than a title and some photographs of Nordstrom people. The other side has a very simple prescription for success in the job: "Use your own good judgment in all situations." Figure 7–4 shows the complete text of the employee handbook. Contrast it with the kinds of bureaucratic manuals handed out by many companies, which run to many pages of rules and regulations.

FIGURE 7–4
Nordstrom Employee Handbook

WELCOME TO NORDSTROM

We're glad to have you with
our Company.

Our number one goal is to provide
outstanding customer service.

Set both your personal and
professional goals high.
We have great confidence in your
ability to achieve them.

Nordstrom Rules:

Rule #1: **Use your good
judgment in all situations.**

There will be no additional rules.

Please feel free to ask
your department manager,
store manager or division general
manager any question
at any time.

nordstrom

A service culture begins with the leadership of the company. It survives and thrives through the continuing attention and care of the managers at all levels. And it pays off in the feelings and actions of the frontline people who *are* the product.

NOTES

[1]Jan Carlzon, *Moments of Truth* (Cambridge, Mass.: Ballinger, 1987), p. 67.
[2]Karl Albrecht, *The Creative Corporation* (Homewood, Ill.: Dow Jones-Irwin, 1987).

CHAPTER 8

INTERNAL SERVICE:
EVERYBODY HAS A CUSTOMER

Where do you go to complain about the complaint department?

—*Laurence J. Peter*
Creator of the Peter Principle

IF YOU'RE NOT SERVING THE CUSTOMER . . .

"If you're not serving the customer, you'd better be serving someone who is."[1]

This bold statement, which is the most often quoted line in *Service America!*, refers to the concept of *internal service*—providing service to the servers, the customer-contact people who take care of the paying customers. It implies teamwork and cooperation all across the organization to make sure service quality stays high.

Many executives and middle managers have quoted this line to me, and I find it intriguing to hear people quote me to myself. The line and the concept behind it have a powerful appeal for many organizational leaders. Many have said, "This, in a few words, is exactly what I've been trying to get across to the people in this organization. I want them to realize that they're all in the service business, not just the ones who deal directly with the customer." The internal service concept is an appealing idea, and it makes good sense as a motif for improving the internal workings of any service business.

Just as the production of a Hollywood movie requires on-camera actors to read lines and act out their parts, the behind-the-scenes people play an equally critical role. If no one is there to build the sets, make the costumes, set up the lights, operate the cameras, activate the microphones, and do the thousands of other things that go into a successful production, the whole show comes to a halt.

The same thing is true of service. In a service business, the actors are the contact employees. They are the ones "on stage," dealing with the customers. But their success depends on the contributions of all the behind-the-scenes employees who have to do many things to assure the frontline service quality. The contact employees are the "customers," so to speak, of the support people. In this sense, all employees are frontline employees, even if there is a distinction between contact employees and "back room" employees. They are all performing service jobs, either for the customers or for one another.

Each group relies on the other to keep the ship afloat, to recall the shared fate metaphor of the previous chapter. Without help from the people who work at the internal levels of the organization, the customer-contact people couldn't do their jobs properly. And the contact people can usually help the support people do their jobs as well. There must be an effective partnership between the people out front and those in the back room for the whole service organization to function effectively.

In a truly service-driven organization, everybody and every unit has a customer. If you or the members of your unit never see the customers, you still have customers of your own. Your customers are the people who depend on you, wholly or in part, to get their jobs done. All of the functions and departments of a service business are interlinked, and each one depends on others to various degrees in accomplishing its mission.

In fact, we can argue that the entire purpose of the organization, indeed its *only* purpose, is to support the efforts of the frontline people to do their service jobs.

Some managers of internal units have a hard time accepting the idea that they are in the service business, that they have customers. I usually offer a standard answer when a manager says, "I don't have customers. I run the accounting department," or, "I run the power generation department." I usually say, "If you don't think you have a customer, there is a simple little test you can perform. Stop doing what you're doing for about three weeks. See who rises up to put the heat on you: that's your customer. Whoever will be unhappy if you don't make the contribution you're supposed to be making is your customer. If you don't hear anything after three weeks, maybe you're not as indispensable as you thought. Take the hint and go to the local print shop with a fresh copy of your resumé, because they're going to catch up with you sooner or later."

If you're a manager, you can also think of your employees as your customers. They need help from you to get their jobs done. You can be service oriented toward your employees as well as service oriented toward your customers.

THE INTERNAL SERVICE TRIANGLE

In *Service America!* and earlier in this book, I refer to the service triangle. Each part of this triad of relationships represents a critical element of the service management concept. It shows the service strategy, the customer-oriented frontline people, and the customer-friendly systems as working together to bring quality service to the customer, who occupies the center position of the triangle. Just as we need the service triangle to help people think about and communicate about external service quality, so we need an *internal service triangle* to help them deal with internal service quality.

The internal service triangle is an exact mirror of the external service triangle, as shown in Figure 8–1. But in place of the paying customer at the center, it portrays the *employees* as the customers of management, and it shows that three critical elements are necessary to win their commitment to serving the external customer:

1. Culture.
2. Leadership.
3. Organization.

The top-most point of the internal service triangle refers to the culture of the organization. *Culture,* for the employee, is the

FIGURE 8–1
The Internal Service Triangle

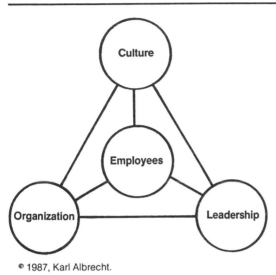

© 1987, Karl Albrecht.

counterpart of service strategy for the external customer. It is the basic message of service that must be there to enable people to make the necessary personal commitment to service quality for the customer.

The bottom-right point of the triangle shows that employees need *leadership* from their managers. Leadership gives the employees the same thing they give to the external customer: personal, caring attention to their needs as people.

And the bottom-left point of the triangle, the *organization,* gives the same thing to the employees that the service systems give to the customer: support.

If top management wants to foster a sense of teamwork and internal effectiveness in the organization, the internal service triangle can help to project the message to all managers of the internal units. The culture, the leadership, and the organization must conspire synergistically to make frontline employees maximally effective. The internal service people can line up their resources behind the external service people, who have to see to it that everything goes right for the customer at the moments of truth.

HELPING SUPPORT DEPARTMENTS
UNDERSTAND THEIR ROLES

The basic idea of internal service is immediately appealing to most managers, but many of them find it quite a challenge to apply the service management model to their own departments. The idea of dealing with other departments as if they were customers is one of those whack-on-the-head ideas that startles people at first. When they begin to work with it, they often discover it's not so easy as it looks. They may have to overturn some of their oldest and most cherished assumptions about what they and their employees should be doing every day.

If the chief executive wants the various department managers to implement the service management philosophy internally as well as externally, it is necessary to help them analyze their operations from this new point of view. They need a prescription for engineering excellent internal service, just as the overall organization needs a prescription, as presented in later chapters. The following discussion offers a general plan for orienting or reorienting an internal service department to its mission.

Defining Your Customer

Some managers of internal service departments can immediately identify their customers. Their interactions with their internal customers may be clearly defined and easy to analyze. But in other cases, the unit's mission may be very broad. It may not be easy to identify a single customer or type of customer whom the department serves. And in either case, the people in the department may need help in thinking through their relationships with their customers and figuring out how to serve them most effectively. Sometimes it takes a careful thinking process and a bit of internal market research to get a clear picture of an internal department's mission and quality criteria.

If you're an accounting department manager, then you know the managers and supervisors in various parts of the organization rely on you for reports, advice, and guidance. If you're a manager in a sales department, then you know the marketing people rely on you for feedback, sales figures, and sales news.

If you are the data-processing systems manager, you have a number of customers spread out all over the company. The people in payroll, personnel, accounting, engineering, finance, and production all use your computer systems and your expertise to help them run their departments. In effect, you're in constant contact with dozens of customers every day. You may never see a single outside customer, but that doesn't mean the people who come to you as internal customers don't need to have their needs met by you in the same effective manner as a customer-contact service person works for the outside customers.

By first identifying these types of cross-relationships—your internal customers who rely on you and others like you to get their work done—you can start to form a more accurate concept of your internal customer population.

Here are some steps you can take to help you get a clearer definition of your internal customers and to develop a service mission for your department:

1. Make a list of all the people or departments in the organization who need help from you or your department in any way; this may include specific departments, particular staff people, the chief executive, certain specific executives, or the board of directors.

2. Prioritize the names on that list, with the people or departments that rely on you the most at the top.

Identifying Your Contribution

3. For each of the customers on your list, specify the primary need you think they have that you can contribute to. Consider some of your own expertise or the resources available in your department as a means of helping your customers meet this primary need. Ask yourself the question from their points of view, not necessarily your own. What are their missions? What are they trying to accomplish? What are their criteria for their own service excellence? What unsolved problems do they face? What makes life difficult for them? Try to relate each of these factors to some aspect of your own organizational mission.

Defining Service Quality

4. Next, for each of your customers, try to define the customer interface in terms of the moments of truth that customer experiences with the service you provide. Make them very specific and concrete. For each moment of truth, try to pinpoint a specific quality factor that you believe the customer considers critical to the successful performance of the service involved. Remember that a moment of truth is any episode in which a customer comes into contact with any aspect of your department, and thereby has an opportunity to form an impression of your service quality. Pick out a few critical moments of truth for your special attention. Choose from those few incidences where you really have to come through to meet the special needs of one of your customers. The other moments of truth you list are also important, but these few extra-effort incidents are critical to your success as a service provider.

5. For each major internal customer, draw up a customer report card, a set of evaluation criteria for your department's service package, as seen through the eyes of that customer. The criteria might include timeliness, reliability, accuracy, technical expertise, the value of your information, or the direct cost, if any, of your service. This is your preliminary prescription for service quality, broken down by the various customer factions you serve.

Validating Your Criteria

6. Next, go and talk with your customers and ask them to look at your draft criteria for service quality. After all, their perceptions are the ones that really count. Ask them to discuss their needs and problems with you in relation to the specific assistance you provide to them. Use these discussions to revise and finally validate the quality criteria on your service report card. One of your first questions to each of these people should be, "What needs do you have that I may be neglecting?" Ask that question and be prepared to sit up and take notice of what you may be missing. You may get a real earful in these sessions but that should be what you really wanted. Through these frank discussions, you may be able to pinpoint specific problems that escaped you previously. The dialogue is the important part. Hearing from the individual department heads might give you a whole new perspective on your department's role in the company.

Conduct a Service Audit

7. Now you're ready to conduct a *service audit* of your organization, by evaluating your service against the quality criteria you established in talking to your customers. Get a fix on the present state of your service quality and identify any immediate opportunities for improvement. Follow through by setting up a process for periodically reviewing the quality of your service or support to the various other units and looking for ways to improve it.

Develop a Mission Statement

8. Finally, once you have a clearer idea of your department's role and contribution, consider drafting a service mission statement for your operation. Make it brief, to the point, meaningful, nontrivial, and comprehensive. Share it with the people who report to you and make sure they fully understand it. Have regular meetings with them to evaluate your service quality, and remind them at each meeting about the priorities defined in your mission. Make sure they see themselves as fully responsible for making the moments of truth come out well for their internal customers, just as the contact people are expected to manage the moments of truth for the external paying customers.

One very strong word of caution is in order regarding defining service contributions by internal departments. Again and again I've seen department heads fall into the trap of trying to define their service in terms of what they *do* instead of what they *contribute*. A manager of an accounting department, when asked, "What is the contribution your group makes to the rest of the organization?" is likely to say, "We handle the accounting system; we pay the bills; we invoice customers; we balance the books; we create the balance sheet and the income statement." All of these may be important, worthwhile *activities,* but the statement doesn't tell what the *contribution* is.

The distinction between activities and contributions seems subtle at first, but it can be critically important in deciding which services are most valuable and what the priorities are. For example, the director of training in one large organization first described her contribution as "effective training programs." After a great deal of thought and discussion, she arrived at a much simpler definition of her unit's contribution: "competent people." There can be a huge difference in the implications of the two definitions. And the means may change radically.

For example, if the contribution is training programs, then the means for making the contribution is to design, create, and implement training courses of various types. If the contribution is competent people, the training director sees her mission much more broadly and starts thinking in terms of options like skills assessment, career development, employee counseling, correspondence study, professional conferences, and support for external degree programs. Competent people might also include the executives, and the training department might undertake executive development programs as part of its contribution.

The same thinking process can apply to virtually all internal service departments. It's important to stretch your thinking beyond the familiar definition of what you do every day and identify the reasons you do it. How do you make the world a better place by doing what you do? What is the ultimate benefit of your outputs? This line of thinking can lead to some very constructive new ways of looking at internal service.

ORGANIZING FOR INTERNAL SERVICE

In some companies, the internal service concept can get executives thinking about new or different ways to structure the organization. By thinking of all the internal service people as aligned in support of the contact people who manage the moments of truth, they may decide some different structural approaches might make sense.

The new, postregulatory AT&T, for instance, has done some very broad rethinking of its structure for service. One result was the decision to centralize a great number of internal services formerly scattered all over the giant organization's landscape. AT&T senior management created a single unit, the Contract Services Organization, chartered to handle support functions like purchasing, personnel management, training and development, facilities management, graphic arts, and a host of others.

According to Bill Ebben, the AT&T vice president and general manager of the Contract Services Organization, "We have to serve the needs of many AT&T organizations and people effectively and competitively. In many cases, our AT&T customers have the option of purchasing services from sources outside the company if they choose. We have to compete for their business, and we have to offer a level of service they can't find elsewhere."

On a smaller scale, many organizations might benefit from reexamining their structural approaches to service delivery. In some cases, it even makes sense to rethink the structure of the parts of the organization that deal directly with the customers. If, for example, the organization tends to give the customer the runaround, or the customer has a hard time figuring out how to deal with the organization or whom to contact, or if the customer has to embark on a research project to figure out how to get his or her needs met, it may be time to think about how you're organized. If the customer experiences too many handoffs or has to cross too many departmental boundaries, you may be structured for your own convenience rather than for the convenience of the customer.

NOTE

[1]Karl Albrecht and Ron Zemke, *Service America! Doing Business in the New Economy* (Homewood, Ill.: Dow Jones-Irwin, 1985), p. 106.

CHAPTER 9

HOW TO IMPLEMENT A
SERVICE MANAGEMENT
PROGRAM

Sooner or later, all the thinking and planning has to degenerate to work.

—Peter F. Drucker

IS YOUR ORGANIZATION READY FOR A SERVICE INITIATIVE?

The road to service excellence is strewn with the debris of ambitious corporate programs that were supposed to revolutionize their organizations, put them on the map competitively, and confer the benefits of quality leadership in their industries. "We're going to be the best in this industry," the executives declared. "Service excellence is the future of this company." "We're going to revolutionize this business, with a standard of excellence no one else can match."

The desire is there and the intention is honorable, but often the organization is just not ready to undertake the venture. The mistakes and pitfalls explained in previous chapters can derail any effort if the right conditions are not in place. No organizational situation will be perfect, of course. There will always be practical problems and factors that can get in the way. But by making an honest assessment of the state of affairs at the outset, we can determine whether success is in the cards. If it is not, and if we believe a service positioning is valid and important, then we must deal with the matter of readiness first. We must remove the major obstacles before trying to launch a service initiative.

If the necessary components for success are not in place at the start, then launching a service program becomes a matter of developing the organization itself as part of the program. This is virtually always the situation to some extent. Becoming customer driven and service oriented usually involves transforming the organization to a degree. But sometimes the organization itself needs major repairs before a major program can work.

If you are thinking about launching a service initiative, you need to ask yourself carefully, calmly, and objectively: Are we ready to do this? At the very least, you need to ask: Can we get ready? Can we develop the organization as we go? The two main components of readiness are a strong executive team, which can carry the program out to the people in the organization and win their credibility and commitment, and a strong, healthy culture, which will support the values and beliefs behind a service commitment and will nurture the program as it grows and develops.

BEING REALISTIC: TIME, ATTENTION, AND RESOURCES

We have already established that wishing for service excellence won't make it happen. We know that taking a normal, reasonably healthy organization from a so-so level of service, i.e., Level 3 as described in Chapter 1, to an outstanding level, such as Level 5, is a big undertaking. But do we really know how big? There is big, and there is *big*. The giants of service, the Level 5 companies that have become legendary for the quality of their service products, have a great deal invested in their cultures, both psychologically and financially. They didn't just write a check one day and buy service excellence. They have been making the investment in it for many years. It's a huge investment when you add it all up, but they believe it pays.

A major organizational transformation is on a par with turning the Queen Mary (in the days when it would turn); it takes a tremendous input of energy, sustained for quite a period of time. And a ship the size of the Queen Mary doesn't turn on a dime either. It takes miles, and it's a very broad turn. Even a small- or medium-sized organization needs time and attention if its leaders want it to change its ways substantially.

The recipe for a service transformation includes three basic ingredients:

1. Time, energy, and effort by its executives and managers.
2. Patience and perseverance by everyone.
3. Money.

The first two ingredients require only the willingness of top management to work hard; the third is usually another matter. The top people have to decide whether they are willing to put up the dough to make it happen. This is really the number-one apprehension factor in most of the corporate service ventures I have observed or participated in, so let's go right to the point and be realistic about what's involved.

There is no exact price tag at the outset that tells you how much it's going to take to get to the promised land. But you'd better prepare yourself for a fairly major investment—major in terms of the kinds of funds you're accustomed to putting up for other major business ventures. A major service commitment can be on a par with launching a new product or product line, opening a new facility, or relocating headquarters. Medium-sized organizations can be in for six-figure investments over several years. Very large organizations are probably looking at multi-million-dollar investments. Small organizations are less hard hit because the cost of communication is generally less for them.

This question of resource investment can really challenge the executive thinking process. Even if you knew exactly how much the venture would cost, you wouldn't know for sure if it would confer a significant competitive advantage. Ultimately, the decision to undertake a service quality program is a matter for executive judgment. If you believe a service focus is critical to the positioning you want for your business, then you have to be willing to put down the chips and go for it.

RECONCILING SERVICE QUALITY WITH COST REDUCTION

One of the most-asked questions in executive seminars on service management is, "Is it possible to make a service quality program work in a situation where you have to keep resources under control, or even cut costs drastically?" It's a tough question, but I believe it has a legitimate answer. The short answer is: Yes. The longer answer may not be as appealing, however.

The cost-quality issue faces all businesses to some extent. I don't know of any firm that can devote lots of money to improving service quality without having to pay significant attention to revenues and costs. Some are better off than others, of course, but they are all in essentially the same boat.

Boston Edison Company, for example, undertook a major wall-to-wall service program simultaneously with a very stringent cost-reduction effort. Initially, they planned to launch the service initiative after completing the major resource-reduction phase. But as the senior executives began to prepare managers for the service program, they found that the two efforts seemed fundamentally contradictory to them. Most of them felt initially that they could not possibly improve service quality after having to give up substantial resources beforehand.

The company's executives decided to retime the events of the two programs and to subordinate the cost-reduction effort to the service initiative. In other words, the managers would make their resource decisions in the context of trade-offs involving cost and quality. There were certain hard realities concerning staff levels and revenue estimates, but the idea was to look for ways to maximize service quality at the same time they were rethinking resource levels.

In the process, they restated an old slogan, and the result made much more sense to the managers. Whenever top management talks about resource reductions, somebody is sure to bring out the old cliche, "We've got to do more with less." In some organizations, it has evolved to "Do more with nothing." I believe that particular catch phrase instills a sense of despair rather than determination in people, especially managers. Boston Edison permanently rephrased the statement and used it as a guiding idea for service quality:

We've got to do better with less.

The Hartford, an old and established insurance company, faced a similar situation. In an executive strategy retreat, the senior managers wrestled with the relationship between a cost-reduction program currently underway and the idea of a major service initiative. They also embraced the idea of doing better with less and decided to search for opportunities to streamline and improve customer service while eliminating unnecessary processes. According to President Don Frahm, "It's clear to me that service is the business we have to be in. Cost reduction is a short-term thing we have to do, but service is the long-term thing we have to do. We have to make the two of them compatible, not only in our own minds, but in the minds of all of the managers out there."

Many organizations are facing the need to control costs and use resources more carefully, even in the best of times. But it is important to recognize the difference between strategy and tactics. The idea of doing better with less suggests that cost reduction is not a strategy, but a tactic. A service focus is the strategy; reducing costs is one of many things we do to implement the strategy. If resources are tight, we have to make some tougher trade-off decisions, but the situation is not qualitatively different because of that. Service excellence is still the long-term goal.

There is good evidence that businesses can indeed achieve superior levels of service during difficult periods of resource reduction. Santa Monica Hospital Medical Center launched a service quality program when the institution was heading into a period of declining patient census and a no-growth demographic trend in its service area. The organization weathered successive budget cuts and two staff layoffs, but it held to the strategy of making its moments of truth as positive as possible by capitalizing on and extending its traditional orientation as a friendly, caring hospital. It was not easy by any means, and the process left the inevitable scars and side effects in terms of employee stress and morale problems.

But, according to President Leonard LaBella, service management provided a guiding model to help people understand what they were going through and keep their attention focused on service quality as the hospital's best strategy for dealing with difficult times. According to LaBella:

> The letters I'm getting from patients and their family members now are amazing. We always did fairly well in that regard, but there's a qualitative difference in the tone and feeling of them. They give specific examples and name names of the nurses and support people they've been so impressed with. Not only that, our scores on the statistical measures of patient satisfaction, doctor satisfaction, and staff commitment are the highest they've ever been. And we've been able to achieve this during one of the toughest periods in our history.

Scandinavian Airlines' Jan Carlzon cites a typical example in which cost reduction and better service went hand in hand. The SAS branch in Stuttgart, Germany, operated out of two locations, one downtown and the other at the airport. Most of the managers worked out of the downtown office, which also handled ticket sales. The airport facility experienced fluctuations in workload among both the passenger and cargo operations. The newly appointed branch manager, Werner Tarnowski, decided to close the downtown office and relocate everyone to the airport. During the process, he crosstrained the passenger and cargo people, so they could balance out the ups and downs of the workload among themselves.

The result was a significant savings in the cost of the operation with no sacrifice in the quality of service. "In fact," notes Carlzon, "service is probably better, because the organization is more flexible."[1]

Cost and quality are not particularly the best of friends, but neither are they necessarily mortal enemies. It is important in launching a service program to give the people in the organization a clear idea of what's happening and to help them see the upcoming changes as falling within the overall umbrella concept of service quality. Sometimes this can challenge the communication and leadership skills of the senior managers. In these situations, it is important to use the principles of good *change management* to make sure the program rolls out in a reasonably constructive way.

A PRIMER ON CHANGE MANAGEMENT

"People don't like change." This is one of those thought-stopping slogans that sound good and are fun to say. But like many slogans, it loses its meaning when one analyzes it carefully. More than anything else, it expresses the frustration that many executives and managers feel when they try unsuccessfully to inflict or induce significant change in human systems. When they discover that people are not excited about whatever they were supposed to get excited about, executives are tempted to blame the people for not wanting to change—for not knowing what is good for them. This is like the physician blaming the patient for not getting well, when the treatment itself is not effective.

Bringing about change in organizations is one of the least understood aspects of management, and it will have to become much better understood for service commitment to become a way of life in more businesses. In these days when so many businesses are facing environmental change and are trying to find themselves, the management of the organization becomes more and more the management of change. Here are some thoughts and suggestions about change and change management.

First, let's stop assuming that people don't like change. It makes more sense to say that people don't like a particular change when they don't think the change will benefit them. People, for the most part, neither like nor dislike change per se. They simply like or dislike the consequences they perceive as being associated with the change. When efforts at change management fail, it is usually because one small group of people decides to try to change the behavior patterns of another group—usually a larger one—without proper regard for the need to provide a benefit premise for the new way of behaving.

Organizational theorist Robert Mager calls this the you-really-oughta-wanna syndrome. The change makers proceed from some kind of evangelical conviction that the changees *should* want to change. If they don't, then they are misbehaving. They are being stubborn, inflexible, and backward. This point of view often leads the changers into trying to bully or shame the changees into going along with the change, rather than building the change premise around a perceived benefit to the changees. In the words of poet

William Blake, "A man convinced against his will is of the same opinion still."

Some simple strategies can bring about change by hooking into the need systems and perceptions of the people in an organization. These change management strategies typically require a great deal of flexibility on your part because they require you to adopt an approach that you can leverage off of the need system of the changee, not the changer. Here are some simple rules of change management.

Stack the deck in favor of acceptance. Ask yourself, "Does the organizational change I have in mind really have benefits for the people who have to adopt it, or am I trying to kid myself as well as them?" Be willing to *change the change,* if necessary, to include elements that have undeniable value to the people most affected. Get those benefits well forward in everyone's perceptions of what's going to happen. Don't expect them to accept some vague, abstract higher purpose as a reason for giving up something they're accustomed to and going to something strange and different. Create basic, concrete, gut-level benefits.

Do it in palatable bites. Except for certain rare, cataclysmic changes best brought about in one stroke, most large-scale changes tend to cause too much disruption and confusion for too long when implemented in one piece. You need to segment the change somehow into smaller steps that flow logically one from another. Think of it as presenting an appetizer, one or more main courses, and the dessert. Just as you wouldn't serve a large meal by putting everything on the table at once, you will have a better result by having things flow in a perceptible natural order. The old expression may be corny but it's still true: "Yard by yard it's hard, but inch by inch it's a cinch."

Outflank the grapevine. Rumors and false stories can sabotage even the best-intentioned of programs if people don't have accurate, trustworthy information about what's going to happen. I've lost count of the organizational programs I've seen that failed or floundered because the changers didn't make the effort to help people understand what they were throwing at them. Fear is an amazing thing. It feeds on the slightest evidence of danger, doom, or disaster. Top management can discuss a plan to change the compensation system in the company one day, and the next day the word will be spreading to all corners of the organization, riding on the same horse with all manner of warnings of dire things to come. Some vice president is going to be fired. The union contract is being violated. Fraud is suspected. All secretaries will be put into one common typing pool. There will be no more department heads. On and on it goes. The only way to outflank the grapevine is to provide information, and plenty of it on a frequent basis, that is more accurate and more reliable than the grapevine provides. This is usually not as difficult as it may seem. But bear in mind that the grapevine carries information that is *personally* important to people, not administrative facts and figures. You must provide the same kind of information, with the same value.

Facilitate each step. At each step in an incremental change process, there are usually a few things you can do to help things along. A key meeting or presentation to employees, publication of an information sheet or status update, or information passed along through supervisors or union representatives tend to eliminate the feeling of strangeness and uncertainty. Getting agreement about how to proceed among key organizational leaders or people who are centers of influence can create leverage with the others. These people, once sold on the process and feeling instrumental in it, can sell the others. Sometimes it helps to have a listening session, in which employees can voice their concerns, raise issues for management consideration, and get answers to their questions. People seldom question management's right to make changes in the organization, but they do feel entitled to have their needs and feelings considered.

Tie a bow around it at the end. There is a certain value in ritual and ceremony. Some executives understand this, but many others have never thought about it. We human beings need to ceremonialize the key changes in our lives. That's why we have weddings, funerals, baby showers, baptisms, bar mitzvahs, graduations, retirements, bachelor parties, house warmings, and grand openings. There is some deep-seated creature need to put handles on major life changes so we can deal with them psychologically as well as logistically. If you recognize this human fact, you can put it to good use in the management of organizational change. At each major milestone in a long-term change process, it helps to gather people together and say or do something in a ceremonial way that makes the change conscious, real, and permanent. When they have reached the ultimate goal, the executives—the authority figures in the tribal society—should present some public event of appropriate magnitude and psychological tone that will bring everyone into the same feeling of completion. This event acknowledges the new reality and makes it the normal state of affairs for the future.

To simplify this idea of change management even more, think of it in three basic steps:

1. *Conceptualize*. Know what you're trying to change.
2. *Incrementalize*. Break it into palatable bites.
3. *Ceremonialize*. Make it culturally permanent.

In undertaking a major program like a service quality initiative, it helps to pinpoint the impact you want the program to have on the organization. What aspects of life, work, and operations need to change? How do they need to change? What stands in the way of the changes, and what can you capitalize on to help the changes along? Then define the exact nature of the overall change you want to bring about. Apply the principles described above—conceptualize, incrementalize, and ceremonialize.

A well-thought-out change management approach, combined with a good measure of realism and a dash of patience, can play a valuable part in the success of any service program.

A MODEL SERVICE MANAGEMENT PROGRAM

There are many ways to go about service quality programs and many imaginative ways to get managers and employees involved. But some common elements do seem to play a part in virtually all successful ventures of this type. Over and above the many options available for the tactical implementation, there seems to be a common flow of events that is important. In observing and participating in a fairly large number of organizational efforts to develop service quality, I have come to rely on a basic five-stage model for keeping the big picture in sight. This simple phased approach, together with a few key implementation strategies, seems to offer a fairly reliable framework for getting the job done.

This model assumes the executives of the company have made a personal commitment to service excellence as the marketing thrust of the business, and they are ready to make the proper programmatic commitment. They are willing to stay with it for the two to three years or more it will normally take to see substantial, permanent results.

A part of the implementation strategy I almost always recommend is formation of a service quality task force to operate as a center of advocacy for the effort. A task force, if well appointed, well developed, and well led, can have a number of advantages. First, it keeps the ball rolling. The executive management team can do only so much to push the program. In a typical fairly large company, the executives may have heavy demands on their time and may find it very difficult to get together often enough to guide the effort in any detail. It is important that the program keep rolling all the time, not just when they can sit down and work out the next steps.

A second advantage of the task force is that it brings the focus of action down at least one level in the organization and begins to make it part of the operational reality. It is also possible to get the support and contributions of people all over the organization, including the rank and file if appropriate. By setting up a stratified task force, i.e., one with members from all levels of the hierarchy and all significant special-interest areas, you can make sure all of the significant issues and points of view get the consideration they deserve.

Another advantage is that the task force makes the service quality program highly visible and credible to the organization because people see their own peers getting involved and making things happen. There is a transfer of ownership from top management to the action people in the organization, and this usually makes the program more believable.

It is generally a good idea, in my view, to have the task force in place and properly developed at the outset of a service program. It is also important that the members understand their mission well, have a personal commitment to it, and have the benefit of a strong chairperson who can provide the energy and leadership necessary to help them accomplish the mission.

FIGURE 9–1
Flow of Events in a Typical Service Quality Program

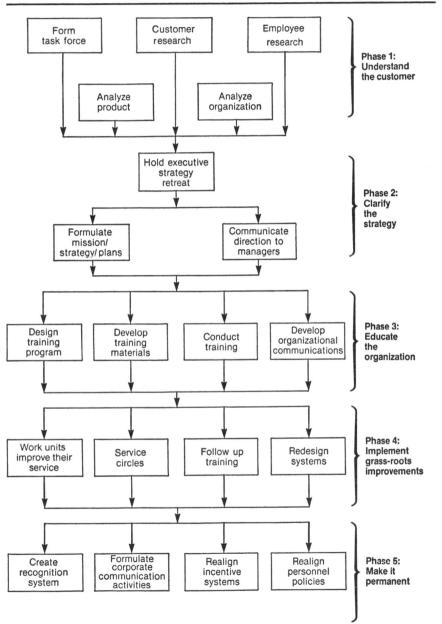

With these preconditions assumed, let's look at the five basic phases of a service quality program:

1. Understand your customer.
2. Clarify your service strategy.
3. Educate the organization.
4. Implement grass-roots improvements.
5. Make it permanent.

The following chapters deal with each of the key phases in turn. These five phases do not have to be completely separate from one another on the time line. They flow into one another and may in some cases overlap or proceed simultaneously, depending on the needs of the organization. In your thinking process, you might choose to divide the process into more or fewer than the five steps shown, but you will probably still come out with some variation of this overall flow of events.

Figure 9–1 on page 155 gives a more detailed picture of the five phases in terms of the actions that typically go on in each of them.

NOTE

[1]Jan Carlzon, *Moments of Truth* (Cambridge, Mass.: Ballinger Publishing Company, 1987).

CHAPTER 10

PHASE 1:
UNDERSTAND YOUR
CUSTOMER

Who the hell wants to hear actors talk?
—*Harry M. Warner, 1927*
Warner Brothers Pictures

The first stage of your service quality program is really a "getting ready" stage. You need to learn enough about the present situation and the opportunities it presents to plan the rest of the program in detail. This first stage involves understanding your customer.

For this discussion, we need to think in terms of *two* "customers":

1. The paying customers.
2. The employees.

You will recall from previous discussions that the service management model sees the employees as your first market, i.e., you have to sell them on the idea of service if you expect them to sell it to the paying customers. In this chapter, we explore what it means to understand both customers.

The following discussion is in two parts: the first deals with understanding the paying customer, and the second part deals with understanding the working customer. As we proceed, you will see how similar the processes are and how interconnected they are in getting to the point of readiness for service excellence.

Let's start with understanding the paying customer.

THE DANGER OF ASSUMPTIONS

The history of innovation in the business world is largely the history of people violating tradition—escaping from the tyranny of long-held assumptions about customers, what they want, what they will buy, how much they will pay, what turns them on, and what turns them off. I said in previous chapters that the longer you're in a certain business, the greater the chances you don't really understand your customer. That's a strong statement, but it becomes a stronger conviction with me almost every day.

When we launched a service quality program at Santa Monica Hospital, we went through a great deal of debate at the outset about the need for market research. Bear in mind that hospitals in general have not had to think in marketing terms over the past 30 or 40 years and that, for most of them, even the concept of marketing seemed like an odd precept for hospitals. Santa Monica Hospital did not have an executive in charge of marketing at that time; it created the position as a result of the thinking process involved in the launch of the service program.

Even though the market research project was not a sophisticated one by any means, it nevertheless disclosed several important findings about both of the hospital's customer groups—the doctors and their patients. Our research revealed that a much higher percentage of patients than expected had a major influence on the decision about which hospital the doctor would use for the surgery or treatment. Formerly, it was a standard assumption that the doctor was the customer and made the admitting decision almost without regard to the patient's preferences. This finding signaled a very significant change in the attitudes of the hospital's customer base and pointed to a very important consideration of marketing strategy, i.e., the need to appeal more directly to the patient-customer. This finding has been documented in other hospital market research, but it was news at that time.

A similar customer surprise came from market research in the cruise line industry. Working with Norwegian Caribbean Lines, one of the major middle-market cruise ship operators serving the Bahamas, I began to wonder about a certain assumption. Virtually all of the competitors in that industry assumed that people who choose ocean-going cruises for their vacations are motivated primarily by a hedonistic desire to indulge themselves in a luxury experience. The desire to be waited on, fed, and catered to seemed to be the central motivator to which most cruise products were trying to appeal. As comedian Jay Leno wisecracked, "Those cruises are something. You get up in the middle of the night to go to the bathroom; you come back and they've made your bed."

I began to believe that something was missing in the thinking process behind cruise marketing when I learned from the existing research that only 4 percent of Americans had ever taken a cruise and that a large fraction of the people who did buy cruises had cruised before. The industry was serving a fairly small segment of the population, and its market was not growing fast enough even to match the general population growth.

The implications of understanding the customer were enormous because even a change of 1 percent of the population, i.e., from 4 percent to 5 percent, would be revolutionary. A great deal of prior research seemed to point to the above-mentioned hedonistic appeal of cruises, yet that 4 percent figure was frustratingly low. During focus-group interviews conducted with people who had never cruised and people who had cruised, we arrived at some interesting insights. Again, many of the findings are confidential, but one in particular stands out as of general interest. This had to do with people's attitudes about food onboard ship.

Most of the cruise advertisements and brochures played up the eating experiences on ship. "Eight meals a day!" the brochures promised. "Sumptuous meals, prepared by world-class chefs!" "Midnight buffet—all you can eat!" A typical cruise brochure showed a groaning board laden with every kind of food imaginable, behind which stood a smiling chef holding a lobster or some other high-luxury item. During the customer interviews, it became obvious that eating is a psychological *double bind* for many people. It was not a solely pleasant prospect for them.

A double bind is a situation in which you have two competing behavioral options to choose from and, whichever one you choose, not choosing the other is going to make you feel bad. Food is a double bind for many people in the following way. A person reads the brochure and sees all that wonderful food. She says to herself (most of the decision makers are women), "Gosh, look at all that food! If I eat that, I'll get fat for sure. On the other hand, I'm paying a lot of money for this experience, so I'd better take advantage of everything they offer." The result is that she feels vaguely uncomfortable and may not even know why. Psychologists tell us that a double-bind situation can arouse feelings of hostility, and, taken to the extreme, it can produce insanity.

This and other findings led to reconsideration of the basic appeal of the cruise product and to new thinking about the very design of the product.

Another company that decided to take a different tack as a result of reexamining assumptions about customers is Host International, a division of the Marriott Corporation that operates airport restaurants, lounges, and gift shops. According to President Ron Johnson:

> All of the research we had seen on airport restaurant customers seemed to say that they felt the food was lousy and the prices were too high. In fact, customers perceived the food quality in cafeteria situations as significantly poorer than the objective quality of the food. Since airport management usually controls the prices we charge, we began looking further into these perceptions of the airport eating experience.
>
> When we looked at our own customer research, something didn't seem to add up. The food was basically high in quality, the environment was clean and attractive, and yet we—and our competitors— were getting low marks overall. We sensed that there was a different interpretation lurking somewhere in the data.

Johnson and his executives asked me to spend a day with them going over the data to see whether we could identify some alternative interpretation that could lead to a differentiating strategy. As we discussed the service product from the customer's point of view, it dawned on us that the perceptions of the eating experience were being distorted, or biased, by the fact that the customers were not necessarily in a positive frame of mind in the service situation. The airport traveler is generally a person under stress. He is out of his familiar environment, often under time pressure, probably fatigued, and perhaps disgruntled as a result of dealing with the hassles of air travel and being away from home. These negative feelings were being projected into the service situation.

Unless the customer was feeling reasonably cheerful and comfortable, he or she would take out the negative feelings on the food-service establishment and would not appreciate the quality of the food or service, no matter how high it might be. This realization led to a special strategy for Host's presentation of the service product to the customer.

According to Host's Ron Johnson, "Most of the firms in the airport service business seem to be selling food. We decided to sell service. We believe that, by offering the customer a total service experience, we may not be able to convert the experience into a dining-out pleasure, but we now know how to add value for the customer and increase the chances that he will appreciate the quality we have to offer."

In quite a few other instances in other industries, customer-research surprises overturned widely held assumptions. Perhaps you believe your industry and your customer are clearly established and well understood. Or you may believe a reconsideration of the whole topic is in order. In any case, it is reasonable to question and reexamine virtually every belief and assumption you have about your customers from time to time. By revising or validating the assumptions on which you base the design of your product and the appeal you make to your market, you can be reasonably sure you are on solid ground. And you can be more confident that you have a meaningful service message to take to the employees of your organization as well as to your customers.

CUSTOMER PERCEPTION RESEARCH

Here follows a brief primer on customer perception research as it applies to service businesses. This discussion won't make you an expert in the subject, but it will equip you to understand what the experts mean when they talk about the subject. The objectives of customer perception research are to identify the characteristics of the service product that are most critical to its acceptance by the customer and to isolate characteristics that can form the basis for successful differentiation of your service product from others in the market.

You can be your own market researcher if you choose, or you can engage the service of a qualified consulting firm. Which of these two avenues you choose depends largely on the level of depth and sophistication you feel is necessary for your program to be on solid ground and on the level of resources you can commit to understanding the customer. By using the basic methods described here, you can stay on fairly safe ground even doing the research yourself.

Three main methods for learning about the perceptions of your customers are:

1. In-depth interviews with individual customers.
2. Focus-group interviews with selected groups of customers.
3. Statistical surveys of representative customer populations.

With all three methods, it is important to select carefully the people from whom you gather the information. They should constitute a reasonably representative sample of the customer population you want to understand. It's usually a good idea to include people who have never bought your service, as well as people who have. It also helps to interview people who prefer your competitor's products as well as those who prefer yours. Disgruntled customers can often tell you as much as happy customers.

How do you reach these customer guinea pigs, and how do you get them to talk to you? There are firms that specialize in customer perception research who can recruit the right people for you, or you can do it yourself if you have the resources. You can recruit interviewees more or less randomly from your customer traffic and the traffic of your competitors. If you want to be a little more sophisticated, you can recruit them by random telephone requests made to a sample of names selected to match the demographics of your customer population.

It is customary to offer the interviewees a small honorarium, say $20, or some small gift to give them an incentive to participate. You can conduct the interviews at some convenient location or in their homes in the case of the individual research.

For questionnaire surveys, you can usually rent a mailing list of names that matches the demographic profile you want to explore.

Each of these three methods has its merits. The method of choice usually depends on what you want to find out. In many programs, each method can play an important role, dovetailing with the others to give a combined picture worthy of management trust.

Use depth interviews with customers when you want to start from scratch and find out how they regard your service product. In a good depth interview, the interviewer takes up to several hours with one person or a family if the family constitutes a singular customer unit. The interviewer asks many questions about all aspects of the service product. This type of interview usually is broad at first and may get more detailed on selected aspects of the subject. The interviewer hopes to uncover key *attributes* of the product that the customers deem important and desirable as well as the *attitudes* the customers hold about those attributes.

For example, if the service product is a public movie theater, the interviewer will probably want to know what makes customers choose to go to a movie over any other way to spend their time. He or she will inquire about prices, showing times, location of the theater, favorite theaters, favorite kinds of movies, whether they usually attend with friends, whether they ever go alone, and on and on.

In the depth interview, the interviewer usually listens for aspects of the experience that people seem to feel strongly about and tries to find out more about the nature of their feelings. There is no intention, or need, in this kind of research to measure anything statistically. The purpose is to identify attributes and attitudes related to the service under consideration.

After a number of interviews, the same answers will start appearing over and over. This is the point at which nothing new seems to be forthcoming and it is reasonably safe to stop interviewing and compile the results. The report from this process usually identifies a number of recurring themes in the customers' statements and tries to tie them to aspects of the product and its delivery. There may be some attempt to prioritize the various perceptual factors as well. The preferred end result is an *attribute list* that defines the total service experience as the customer perceives it.

The second type of research method, the focus-group interview, works much like the individual interviews. The focus group is the method of choice when you want to have people express their views in the company of others. This might be an advantage, for example, when there are various strong views and you want to understand them completely. Conversely, you might choose individual interviews when the subject is rather personal or confidential, such as attitudes and habits about financial investments.

A focus-group interview can range from the very informal to the very sophisticated in terms of technique. The fancier versions use one-way mirrors, closed-circuit videotaping, and exhaustive analysis of the recorded happenings. The informal version is just a get-together between some customers and an astute interviewer/observer. Each method has its devotees; I lean toward the more informal approach in most cases.

The purposes of the focus-group interview are similar to those of the individual interviews, but the discussion technique is, of course, somewhat different. The interviewer tries to involve everyone in the group and tries to draw out various sides of as many issues as possible. If one person states a strong opinion and the others seem to go along with it, the interviewer will probe to see whether opposing views are left unstated. A typical focus-group session takes place at a time and place convenient to the people involved and may last about two hours.

If you are not recording the discussions, it is important to have a skilled observer present, taking notes. If you do record the session, you and others can go over the results in great detail afterward. Just remember that you will probably spend about two to three hours of analysis for every hour of interview tape. It gets pretty tedious watching a couple of hours of round-table conversation over and over, trying to pry out key points.

Finally, you can use a statistical questionnaire survey when you want to gather customer perception information from a relatively large number of people. Individual interviews and focus-group interviews do not generally involve enough people to enable you to make statistically valid judgments about your whole customer base. But they do serve the crucial role of defining the questions you need to ask in your surveys. From the interview process, you can extract a *research model* for the questionnaire phase. A research model is simply a list of key topics you want to enquire about. These key topics include opinions or preferences about the key attributes of the service you are selling, as well as customer demographic information. You can process this information statistically to develop a profile of the service preferences of your customers, possibly their attitudes toward you and your competitors, and a demographic breakdown of preferences by factors like age, gender, educational level, and income level.

If you want to do some customer research on your own, and save the costs of having an outside firm do it, you can use one of the personal-computer software packages on the market, such as *Custometrics,* that process statistical survey data.

The ultimate outcome of customer perception research is a prescription for success in marketing and delivering your service product. The goal is to arrive at a *customer report card* that defines the *key attributes* of the total service experience you are offering. This report card, as explained in the following discussion, serves as your manifesto for managing service quality. The more valid and reliable the report card, the more confident you can be about the design of your service package, the more clearly you can communicate the criteria for excellence to your employees, and the more readily you can measure the quality of your product.

THE CUSTOMER REPORT CARD

The customer report card is a structured presentation of the criteria for service excellence. It interrelates three kinds of information:

1. The key quality attributes of the service.
2. The relative desirability of each attribute to the customer.
3. Your company's scores on these attributes and—if available—your competitors' scores.

Here, when I use the term *service,* I am referring to the total service experience of the customer, which involves all attributes identified in the research. It includes not only the key characteristics of the service itself, but also the characteristics of the delivery process that the customer perceives.

FIGURE 10–1
The Customer Report Card

Critical Factor	Priority	Score
1. Product selection	8	B
2. Price/value	5	A
3. Friendly staff	2	C
4. Quick response	1	A
5. Technical know-how	9	D
6. Etc.	—	—

Figure 10–1 portrays the general structure of the customer report card as a thinking model. Your report card will show the attributes you have identified as unique to your service product.

As a concrete example for discussion, I included in Figure 10–2 the exact structure of a report card used by a small company. Shamrock Press, a publishing arm of my own firm, distributes books, films, software products, and training materials to businesses via direct mail. The staff, taking my service management gospel to heart, wanted to develop their own customer report card and evaluate the quality of their service themselves. Figure 10–2 shows the report card used daily by the staff of Shamrock Press.

In this case, the report card groups the 15 key attributes of the service into four categories: Quality Products, Order Handling, Telephone Service, and Cooperation with the Customer when unusual needs or situations arise. Also, the employees used a high–medium–low classification system for the priority. They chose this method because they felt, from talking with customers, that the various attributes were nearly equal in importance. The use of a "low" priority rating does not imply the factor so rated is unimportant, merely that other critical factors outrank it. If a factor shows up on the report card at all, it is intrinsically important to the customer in some way.

The customer report card starts the thinking process for designing and delivering an excellent service product. You can use it to conduct a *service audit* any time you choose. You can use it as the basic measurement scheme in a regular process of measuring your customers' perceptions of the quality you deliver. And, perhaps most importantly, you can use it as a communication vehi-

FIGURE 10–2
Sample Report Card

Report Card for Shamrock Press		
Service Attribute	*Priority*	*Our Score*
Quality Products:		
Individual product value	High	
Product selection	Medium	
Value for the price	Medium	
Order Handling:		
Reliability	High	
Shipping speed	High	
Accuracy of order, bill, etc.	Medium	
Packaging quality	Low	
Telephone Service:		
Answering speed	Medium	
Friendliness	High	
Helpfulness	High	
Product knowledge	Low	
Efficiency of phone procedure	Low	
Cooperation with the Customer:		
Making things convenient	Medium	
Willingness to compromise	High	
Recovery from errors/mistakes	Low	

cle to help your employees understand how to make a hit with their customers. A valid and reliable report card can serve as the foundation of the entire organizational thinking process about quality.

UNDERSTANDING THE ORGANIZATION AND THE PEOPLE

Now we come to the second customer: the people in your organization. It makes no more sense to go ahead with a service quality program without finding out where the people's minds are than it makes sense to go ahead without understanding the paying customer. You need to make a realistic assessment of the readiness of the organization and the people to undertake the venture you have in mind. This investigation should typically proceed in parallel with the customer perception research process described previously. There are good reasons to get all the research done at the outset and get the findings all in one place so you can make a total assessment of the situation.

In assessing the organization, you can at the very least identify potential blocking factors and potential helping factors. It is a simple and useful thing to do. Hold a meeting of your executive staff, preferably as part of a strategy planning retreat or some other off-site get-together when everyone can tune in to the critical issues without disruption. With the aid of a moderator or trained facilitator, the group can create two lists. Call one "Potential Obstacles" and the other "Potential Assets."

The obstacles are organizational or circumstantial factors that will probably work to oppose or slow down the venture, at least at the beginning. These might include organizational traditions, policies, procedures, norms, rules and regulations, habits, resource limitations, union-management problems, employee attitudes, management attitudes, and current customer perceptions.

The assets list will identify factors already in place that will probably work in favor of the program. These might include a strong executive team, current customer acceptance, an unclaimed niche in the market, cultural norms, organizational traditions, employee attitudes, and so on. Note that factors such as organizational traditions and norms can serve as either obstacles or assets, depending on how they affect the people in your organization.

If you have doubts about any of the obstacles or assets or need to know more about certain aspects of your organization's culture, you can investigate these matters in greater depth using the same kinds of methods used for understanding the paying customers. In other words, you can use in-depth individual interviews, focus-group interviews, and questionnaire surveys to understand the perceptions of the employees just as easily as you used them with the customers.

In fact, it probably makes sense to devote as much attention to assessing employee attitudes as to assessing customer attitudes. You don't want surprises in either area.

QUALITY OF WORK LIFE: MEASURING AND MANAGING FEELINGS

A convenient barometer of culture and climate in an organization is *quality of work life,* or QWL, defined in terms of the perceptions of the employees. High quality of work life involves at least the following factors:

1. A job worth doing.
2. Safe and secure working conditions.
3. Adequate pay and benefits.
4. Job security.
5. Competent supervision.
6. Feedback on job performance.
7. Opportunities to learn and grow in the job.
8. A chance to get ahead on merit.
9. Positive social climate.
10. Justice and fair play.

Each of these 10 factors represents an important aspect of a person's total work experience, i.e., the totality of his or her existence as a member of the organization. Each plays a part in the individual's perception of what it's like to work there.

If you can measure quality of work life, you can manage it, and you can measure it fairly simply. All you have to do is prepare a questionnaire that asks employees to rate their perceptions of the 10 factors, say on a standard 5-point like–dislike scale. Add the basic demographic factors of age, gender, ethnic origin, education level, length of employment, and job classification, and you have a simple questionnaire that can tell you a great deal about the climate in your organization.

It's a good idea to measure QWL on a regular, periodic basis— at least annually—although relatively few organizations do. By keeping the questionnaire brief and simple, you keep the measurement process simple and manageable. You also make it easy for managers to read and interpret the results.

Once you have a profile of QWL as seen by the employees, you can analyze the scores and look for any areas that need attention. Review each of the 10 components of QWL listed above and think about how each one affects the individual employee's motivation and willingness to commit his or her energies to serving the customer effectively. For example, a person who perceives very little opportunity for advancement may find it difficult to put his or her heart and soul into the job. This factor as well as each of the other factors in the QWL model can lead to negative feelings on the part of the employees if it is out of kilter.

A quality of work life assessment gives you both a short-term picture of the situation and any needs for improvement in the climate. It also gives you a longer-term barometer of your success in creating a service culture.

THE NEED TO MEASURE SERVICE

If you hope to make service quality a self-perpetuating phenomenon in your organization, you must "close the loop" with some kind of feedback system that reinforces good behavior. You must establish a process for measuring the quality of the service and making the measurements known to your managers and employees. It won't do to simply preach and teach service and hope everybody does the right things. You must make the whole organization self-correcting and quality-seeking.

The starting point for the measurement of service is the customer report card you discovered during the market research process. The attributes of your service package most desired by your customers must become your guideposts for assessment and correction of the outcomes of the work. Everyone in the organization, from the highest executive to the frontline worker, needs to know what those attributes are and why they are important. It's not enough for the marketing department to know what counts with the customer; everybody needs the information.

There are various methods by which you can gather the feedback data you need to assess your service quality. The method of choice will depend on how you deal with your customers and how your employees operate in their jobs. For example, if your employees contact the customers directly, you can use a simple evaluation questionnaire at the point of contact. If you provide an invisible service, such as in a direct-mail or telephone operation, you might need to use a postal questionnaire. Occasional one-to-one customer interviews can also be helpful, especially in validating the results of questionnaire surveys.

Because your employees are, in a sense, customers too, it makes sense to seek their opinions about the quality of the service. You might want to distribute a questionnaire survey to the staff on a periodic basis to assess their impressions of the service product and to seek their perceptions of the organization's commitment to service.

In some cases, it makes sense to set up a service quality measurement system at the very beginning of the program. In other cases, it might be appropriate to wait until some of the necessary organizational systems are in place, especially if there has not been a tradition of self-measurement and evaluation. But in any case, the puzzle is not complete until you have some regular, periodic, routine measurement process in place and providing quality data to both the managers and the employees.

CHAPTER 11

PHASE 2: CLARIFY YOUR SERVICE STRATEGY

To make a great dream come true, you must first have a great dream.

—*Hans Selye*

CHARTING THE COURSE

The element of *service strategy* has turned out to be one of the most provocative aspects of the service management model. For many companies, it is one of the most difficult and challenging problems to solve. Some organizations face complex circumstances in their business environments and find it difficult to establish a clear-cut market strategy and direction. I don't have all the answers to these questions of strategy and positioning, but in my observation of and participation in the service strategy thinking process in a number of firms in various industries, I have noticed a few key factors that can help the process.

WHAT IS A SERVICE STRATEGY?

What is a service strategy? Why do you need one? And what does it do for you?

A service strategy is a distinctive formula for delivering service; such a strategy is keyed to a well-chosen benefit premise that is valuable to the customer and that establishes an effective competitive position.[1]

In other words, a service strategy is just like a product strategy. You are positioning a service product in its marketplace in the

172

same sense that you would position a conventional physical product. Think about the elements of the definition given above: distinctive formula, benefit premise, valuable to the customer, competitive position. These are the things you decide on when you determine what part of the market you're going to tackle and how. You can't be all things to all people, so you have to decide what you're going to be and to whom. That's what you're deciding when you select your service strategy.

An effective service strategy meets the following criteria:[2]

1. It is nontrivial; it has weight. It must be more than simply a "motherhood" statement or slogan. It must be reasonably concrete and action-oriented.
2. It must convey a concept or a mission which people in the organization can understand, relate to, and somehow put into action.
3. It must offer or relate to a critical benefit premise that is important to the customer. It must focus on something the customer is willing to pay for.
4. It must differentiate the organization in some meaningful way from its competitors in the eyes of the customer.
5. If at all possible, it should be simple, unitary, easy to put into words, and easy to explain to the customer.

In the simplest possible terms, the service strategy answers the question:

Why should the customer choose us?

Some companies can arrive at a clear and compelling service strategy quickly and easily, based on the prospects in their industries. But for many, it's a struggle. It's not always easy to pinpoint a red-hot service strategy at the drop of a hat. Sometimes it takes time, careful review of the customer's interests, and a realistic appraisal of what the organization can do.

For some firms, it seems especially hard because of the structure of their industries or the ways they typically relate to their customers. Sometimes a complete mental block stands in the way of a simple and compelling strategy. But it has been my experience that with a determined attack on the problem, armed with good customer perception research and a bit of imagination, it is usually possible to come up with something that will work well.

Service America! provides a thorough discussion of the rationale and the thinking process involved in clarifying the service strategy, and I commend that discussion to your attention if you feel it would be worthwhile. The present discussion will concentrate more on the actual strategy-setting process itself, in the context of an overall service quality program.

SPECIAL PROBLEMS IN STRATEGY SETTING

Some organizations face particularly difficult circumstances in trying to arrive at a strategy formulation because of the nature of their business. One of the most common problems is lack of differentiation in the basic service product. If your product is basically a commodity in the eyes of your customers and competitors, it is difficult to give it a personality or a special touch. This is often the case with financial services. To most people, a bank account is a bank account; one certificate of deposit is like another—only the interest rate is important; one insurance policy is like another; one individual retirement account is like another.

But to say the product is a commodity is just another way of saying the providers of the product have failed to differentiate themselves in the eyes of the customer. The fact that there is little perceived difference among the competing products can be just as much an opportunity as a handicap. If your competitors are pushing a personality-less commodity at the customer, you may be able to build a significant competitive edge by building a personality into your total service product.

Typically, the place to look in the commodity situation is not the commodity itself, but something to do with the way the customer experiences the product. You need to explore the service context, the key relationships, the unusual situations that come up, the dissatisfiers, and the unrecognized needs customers may have. These are the areas in which you are more likely to find a hidden opportunity for putting something special into the way you do it.

Another special problem area in selecting a service strategy is in the case of an organization that has few clearly identified competitors. This is the case, for example, with most public utilities, especially gas and electric companies. This type of utility usually operates as a natural monopoly, i.e., it enjoys a guaranteed monopoly status conferred by government in exchange for a fully regulated profit structure. Utility executives typically sense the need to become more service oriented in order to maintain a positive public image that can help them when they go through the highly politicized process of rate review.

In such a case, it makes sense to see the service strategy as a business concept that has the promise of getting the results the company needs—favorable public opinion that can disarm most of the more aggressive opponents that have a vested interest in attacking the utility. This usually leads to a total-service-excellence type of strategy, keying on the total customer community, which includes residential ratepayers, commercial ratepayers, local governments and special interest groups, and the public utility regulatory commissions. By dealing with all of these interest groups in a customer-first way, the utility may have a better chance of getting near its allowed rate of return. One of the utility's objectives should be to make itself less of a political football for the press and the special interest groups.

Another confusing situation for service strategy thinking can arise in organizations that have significant anti-customer-service value systems. I mentioned previously the example of some hospitals, in which medical people conceive of what they do as somehow above the crass, commercial level of revenues and profit. Many hospitals still lack a significant orientation toward marketing and competitive thinking. The idea that each person is serving customers ranges from mildly distasteful to offensive to some health-care people. Educational institutions often have this same kind of value conflict. It is very difficult for many academic people to look upon education as a product they create and deliver for a price.

In such a situation, the problem is not one of strategy, but a problem of values. The top managers of such an organization must work on the attitudes that block the transformation in consciousness that must come. It is especially important in these cases to arrive at a service concept and a way of expressing it that is compatible with the strong professional values that exist among the people who will have to implement it.

If you are trying to formulate a service strategy and you don't seem to be getting anywhere, probably the most beneficial action you can take is to go back to the customer perceptions. More often than not, lack of a satisfying strategy points to a lack of adequate market definition. The more intimately you understand your customers and the better you understand what they are trying to buy, the better your chances of identifying a critical positioning factor.

Of course, the world won't come to an end if you don't find a service strategy that turns you on. You've been surviving without one, so you must be doing things basically right. And indeed there is nothing intrinsically wrong with deciding that doing the basics as well as you possibly can is your strategy. But a market position that is distinctively your own can make life much more satisfying. It gives you an organizing principle for the design of your service product; it gives you a clear promise you can take to your market; and it gives you a clear concept for action that you can convey to the people in your organization.

MAKING UP YOUR MIND: THE EXECUTIVE STRATEGY RETREAT

Arriving at a service strategy is a critically important step, and it needs proper attention and participation by all members of the executive team. A strategy concept is more likely to stand the test of time if it arises from a strong consensus among the top leaders. If the chief simply makes a declaration of strategy or direction and spoon-feeds it to the other executives, it may or may not be tasty to them. It might be a great idea, and it might have immediate appeal to all of them. Or it might not make sense to them; they might not be excited about it. On the other hand, if they all play a part in creating it, and all of them have time to think it through and appreciate its merits, they are much more likely to get behind it and sell it to their subordinates.

It is almost always worthwhile for the executives to devote whatever time they need to the process of thinking through the direction. The vision they create must work; it must make sense; it must be compelling; and it must be salable.

My favorite process for formulating or clarifying the service strategy is an executive retreat devoted solely to that objective. In a typical retreat, the executive team goes off site, usually for a full day—more if necessary—and goes through a fundamental, soul-searching process of thinking through the direction of the organization with respect to being in a service business.

The first step in the process is to immerse yourself in the market research data. What does the customer perception research tell you about your customers, your service product, and the products of your competitors? Somewhere in all this information—the interview data, the focus-group results, the questionnaire statistics—may lie hidden a benefit premise of such significant potential value to the customer population you want to reach that you can transform it into the main personality factor for your product. Or it may not be hidden; it might be staring right at you, asking to be recognized. This is what you are looking for in the data: an edge factor.

There is no real formula for this thinking process; it becomes a matter of your own perceptions and realizations about what might constitute a key positioning opportunity. One of my favorite ways to tackle this information immersion is to use creative problem-solving methods such as plastering the walls of the meeting room with information diagrams—"mind maps"—that portray what we know about the customer and the competitive set. Using newsprint sheets and colored markers, we put everything up where everybody can see it. Then we start discussing it, not being too concerned at the outset with discipline or logic. The objective at first is to grasp the meaning of the customer data. The next objective is to come to a realization about what will work with the customer and what won't.

In this process, we need to look at the information with innocent eyes. We must pretend we have never seen it before and take it on face value. Do the research data contradict any of our assumptions, beliefs, or convictions. Are there any holes or confusion factors in the picture? How clear is the message coming from the market? How consistent are the findings?

The next step is to apply a bit of right-brain thinking and try to extract some alternative possibilities for a service strategy. What are the major positioning options? Is price positioning an attractive avenue? Would a premium-price position with tremendous added value sell? Is a high-tech product attractive? Or would a high-touch orientation have a stronger appeal? Does efficiency count? Accuracy? Is customer trust a big factor in perception?

These questions are of course generic. They might not fit your situation completely. But they convey the kind of thinking process that has to go on.

The objective of the second-stage thinking process just described is to create a list of options to choose from in selecting a positioning strategy. In some cases, the whole executive team will fall in love with one particular strategy avenue right away; this is fine, provided that attachment is rational as well as emotional. In other cases, it might become a matter of careful evaluation of several competing options. In any case, the objective of the retreat is to emerge with a service strategy that can serve as the organizing principle for a major service initiative.

Once you have a service strategy you believe in, it's a good idea to subject it to a few test criteria to make sure it's likely to hold up over time. Ask yourself at least the following questions about the strategy you have in mind:

1. Can it clearly differentiate you and your service product from the customer's other choices? Is the benefit premise behind the strategy clear and compelling?
2. Can you commit to it? Is it something all executives can believe in and work to support?
3. Can your organization make it work?
4. Can you communicate it to your customers in very concrete, selfish terms?
5. Can you dramatize it to your organization's managers and employees?
6. Can you make it real operationally? Can you make it concrete and experiential for both the employees and the customers?

A final and very important test of your service strategy is to see whether it is congruent and compatible with the customer report card you developed as a result of your market research. Does the strategy you have in mind zero in on certain critical attributes of the total customer experience? In other words, will the customer pay for it?

Once you have selected or invented a strategy, try to cast it in compelling prose. You might want to give this task to your favorite wordsmiths, or you might want to have the executive group agree on a brief strategy statement. This process also dovetails with the associated processes of drafting a mission statement and forming program objectives and an implementation plan.

THOUGHTS ON MISSION AND STRATEGY STATEMENTS

There are various schools of thought concerning the means executives should use to specify the organization's direction to subordinates. Some organizations use elaborate planning and guidance documents, and others use modest ones. Executive strategy sessions often get into deep water due to lack of consensus about when and how to use things such as mission statements, strategy statements, corporate goals and objectives, policies, strategic plans, and operational plans. Lately, many executives have also been thinking about publishing broad statements of company values, principles, and beliefs.

It's little wonder that confusion sets in because of so many available vehicles for spelling out direction. The media chosen need to fit the overall purpose of getting the organization on the road to a service quality orientation.

There will never be complete agreement among all management theorists and executives on these matters, but there is reasonable consensus on the big picture. When you lay out the direction for your organization, it may be appropriate to revise or even rethink all of your guidance documents to make sure they all transmit the same consistent message.

Let's itemize and define the basic vehicles for corporate direction and see how they relate. The following classification system reflects my own biases and may not correspond exactly with other writers on this subject.

The Mission Statement.   The basic foundation document of the business. Tells what business you're in, what market you serve, what you bring to that market, and in particular the special way in which you approach that market.

Company Values. A set of precepts, principles, beliefs, or statements of advocacy to which top management pledges its adherence. The human factors that drive the conduct of the business. Often published and posted prominently for everyone's benefit.

The Service Strategy. May be contained in the mission statement or in a separate document. Specifies the personality of your service product and explains the unique selling proposition that defines your positioning in your market. It is initially helpful in launching a service quality program, but ideally it should become an intrinsic part of the mission statement and the accepted definition of the service product.

The Strategic Plan. Defines the company's next moves over a period of one to several years. May set forth a few critical *key result areas* (in management-by-objectives style) that guide the development of implementing objectives and the annual tactical planning process. Some executives prefer to set a few major strategic objectives in the strategic plan rather than specify key result areas. The plan is subject to revision or updating on an annual basis, but tends to transcend the annual planning process.

The Annual Business Plan. This tactical plan implements the multiyear strategic direction. It specifies major objectives for the business and tells generally how to achieve them. The plan is broken down by major organizational division or department. Some organizations have only individual unit plans; others aggregate all unit plans into a total planning document.

The Operating Budget. The operating budget spells out expected income levels and anticipated expenses for carrying out the business plan, and it is broken down by organizational unit or major program venture.

Some executives regard these kinds of corporate "charter" documents as motherhood statements of little real value in running the business. This is usually true if they don't arise from clear visionary thinking and if they don't present a valid message about the business imperative. But if they are well thought out and well written, they can focus the attention of managers and through them the attention of the employees on the things that count.

With a clear and valid set of charter documents in place, people in the organization sense that their executives have a clear direction and an appropriate plan, and that they speak with one voice. As we have seen before, this is one of the important conditions that must prevail for people to get turned on about a major initiative based on service quality.

NOTES

[1]Karl Albrecht and Ron Zemke, *Service America! Doing Business in the New Economy* (Homewood, Ill.: Dow Jones-Irwin, 1985), p. 174.

[2]Ibid.

CHAPTER 12

PHASE 3: EDUCATE THE ORGANIZATION

Knowledge itself is power.
—*Francis Bacon*

PREACHING AND TEACHING THE GOSPEL

Some companies seem to have been born with the service commitment deeply ingrained in their cultures. Others—the vast majority—have to learn it. There needs to be a process by which the concept and the commitment of quality service find their way into all the nooks and crannies of the organization. The service orientation must somehow become a basic part of the collective organizational psyche.

This is the objective of the third phase of our model service quality program: to preach and teach the gospel of quality service to all the land and to all the inhabitants thereof. The education phase is the first real test of executive skill in selling service to the people. The first two phases—understanding the customer and clarifying the strategy—involved a relatively small number of people, mostly managers. But the education process must win the attention and interest of a different group of people: the rank and file.

There may not be any real obstacles to acceptance on the part of the employees. They may be ready, willing, and able to buy the idea and make the commitment. But considering how much information they get thrown at them every day and how much top-management propaganda they've heard over the years, it's reasonable to expect to face a challenge in making the message of service quality heard over the racket going on in the organization's communication channels.

The education phase is a communication and persuasion phase. We have to sell the commitment to service excellence; we have to communicate the service strategy; we have to give people the information they need to put the strategy to work in their jobs; and we have to give them the skills they need to handle their service jobs well.

Organizations that excel in service quality typically invest heavily in employee training and in the overall process of communicating quality. For them, the investment is just part of the cost of doing business. Their executives believe training and development of frontline people is nothing more or less than product development. They realize the employees *are* the product for the most part, and they deserve adequate attention to make sure they are the best product possible.

I used to believe that service employees had an instinctive understanding of what quality service is, and that they needed more in the way of personal skills training than strictly job-task training. But I have changed my view to some extent. I now believe many contact employees, particularly the inexperienced and those new to the work force, need to have some pretty clear instruction in what is and isn't quality service.

Case in Point: While waiting for a flight in an airport departure lounge, I watched the following scene. A young gate agent was working alone at one of the counters. She went to the microphone and announced: "Attention, all passengers on Flight XYZ to Santa Maria: your flight has been canceled. Please approach the podium at gate 71–A." The usual hassle ensued, with a (mercifully small) number of angry passengers thronging around the podium.

What was missing in her announcement was any hint of an apology or any trace of concern for the passengers as people. Just "Your flight has been canceled." Take it or leave it, like a slap in the face. Further, her choice of words, which I'm sure she picked up from hearing other gate agents, was interesting: "Please *approach* the podium." It sounded like they were supposed to approach some altar or throne on their hands and knees.

Here was a young, inexperienced service person confronted with a problem she was unprepared to handle. She was probably apprehensive about having to deal with the disgruntled passengers.

She handled the situation the best way she knew how. But there are much better ways, and at that point in her work experience she probably hadn't learned them.

Whoever trained and indoctrinated the young woman for her job left out some advice on how to handle a problematical moment of truth, one that is relatively common in that business. Had she been given some skill and some ideas for recovering from a canceled-flight situation, she and her passengers might have felt much better about the situation.

In our model service quality program, the education phase has two major components: intensive skills training for all of the employees and an intensive organizationwide communication campaign to reinforce the message of the training and keep it alive.

In this chapter, we will see what it means to use wall-to-wall training as a communication process. And we will see what else must be done to carry it through and make the commitment permanent.

WALL-TO-WALL TRAINING: A NEW PHENOMENON

Training directors in most American companies have for years faced a fundamental dilemma. They have been convinced of the value of employee training and the contribution it can make to the effectiveness of their organizations overall. Yet the vast majority of them find it difficult to make a convincing case for significant investments by top management in the training—or "human resources development"—process. Training in most organizations typically operates on a "level of effort" type of budget allocation. That means the funds allocated to training go up or down depending on how well the organization is doing financially. The funding level depends not on any particular objective that the training department is expected to achieve, but rather on the amount of money top management feels it can spare.

This is one reason customer service training has traditionally been a creature of good times and has gone begging when things got rough. Until the service revolution got underway in earnest, most executives simply did not look upon training as a key avenue for dealing with the company's problems.

That state of affairs changed radically with the landmark program undertaken by Jan Carlzon during his spectacular turnaround of SAS. When SAS was losing some $17 million, Carlzon launched a service quality program with 100 percent employee training as the centerpiece of the effort. He decided to invest several million dollars to train every one of SAS's more than 20,000 people. He believed his message was important enough to warrant the investment, and he was convinced it would not trickle down through the layers of the organization if all he did was tell his middle managers how important it was. He wanted the message presented in its original, compelling, unfiltered, undiminished form to every SAS employee.

The SAS program was, to the best of my knowledge, a major turning point in western management. It was the first time I know about when a major corporation used a 100 percent training process as part of a major attempt at cultural change. Every SAS employee, manager, and union representative went through an intensive two-day workshop devoted to "the new SAS." The company contracted with a training services firm, Time Manager International, to conduct the programs. They were large affairs, averaging 100 to 150 people per session, presented by skilled, highly motivational speakers.

Carlzon later repeated the same move, again to further his objectives for the organization. In 1983, as the company's turnaround was well underway, he called in his training people and said, "You know, it concerns me that SAS employees don't really understand the profit picture of the company. I don't think they realize where the money comes from, where it goes, how much it costs to run this company, and what influence they themselves have on profit. I want you to teach them all how to read the balance sheet and income statement of the company."

As a result of Carlzon's determination to have the employees understand their roles in the company's survival and success, each of them attended a one-day training course designed to equip them to read and understand the company's basic financial reports.

Not long after the SAS program made headlines, another major corporation, also in the airline industry, undertook a similar wall-to-wall training program designed to communicate the message of service excellence. British Airways put all 37,000 of its employees worldwide through a two-day program similar to the one SAS conducted. The company even built a special training center outside London to accommodate the European employees in style.

Since the SAS and British Air programs, I have seen a number of other major companies and small ones as well, decide to use 100 percent training as an integral part of service quality programs. I have recommended this approach a number of times as well. For example, at Santa Monica Hospital Medical Center in California, we trained all 1,500 employees in the methods of service management as part of the organizationwide campaign to reorient the hospital to a marketing philosophy based on service quality.

Boston Edison Company, with more than 4,000 employees, recently embarked on a similar program. Every employee will attend one or more training sessions that will provide new skills, new ideas, and new priorities for customer service.

The Sheraton Hotel Corporation plans to train or retrain all of its more than 100,000 employees worldwide to instill the customer-first gospel. According to John Kapioltas, chairman of Sheraton, "We typically spend anywhere from $3 million to $7 million to renovate just one hotel property, to bring it up to our standards of quality. It seems to me the same kind of investment in our people is warranted, to make sure they're prepared to provide the same level of service quality we promise to our customers."

We now seem to be in the era of wall-to-wall training as a major corporate method for bringing about high-quality service. More and more senior executives are using the training function as an instrument of policy to mass communicate the message of service quality to their organizations.

METHODS AND OPTIONS FOR TRAINING

The method of choice for delivering training will depend on the nature of the organization, its people, and the message it is supposed to deliver. The basic two-day workshop format is a popular one for good reasons. It is intensive, in that it concentrates a lot of ideas and skill-building processes in a short time. Two straight days of concentrating on a subject embeds it deeply in people's minds. By the end of the second day, things really begin to soak in.

The two-day format is often logistically convenient as well. The employees may work at a number of scattered locations, making it impractical to bring them together repeatedly for short-session courses every week or month. Depending on the training design and the skills of the trainer, trainee groups can consist of 50 to 100 people. Some trainers argue that effectiveness diminishes radically when the group size gets much above 30, but my experience show it is possible to work effectively with groups much larger than that and still maintain a format of practical workshop activities and sharing of experiences.

Some businesses, however, simply cannot take large numbers of people away from their jobs at the same time; the operation would come to a halt. In a hotel, for example, the service would deteriorate quickly if the whole staff, or even a majority, were to spend two whole days in training. Restaurants have the same problem. In cases like these, it is more practical to train people in small groups for short periods of an hour or two and to spread the training over several weeks or months. Often the local manager, i.e., the hotel manager or the restaurant manager, has to serve as the trainer because of the prohibitive expense of having a professional trainer keep visiting the site for so many short sessions.

Some organizations prefer to use small-unit training programs based on the individual work group. In these cases, the training experts design and produce self-study materials for use by the unit supervisors and their people. Such a set of materials might consist of an audio or videotape, a loose-leaf-bound leader's guide, overhead transparencies, and workbooks for the employees. The unit leader would have a lesson guide to follow, with all of the activities spelled out in detail.

The content of the training is just as important as the means for delivering it, and usually more so. Customer service training today is moving away from the old "smile training" discussed in previous chapters and toward the kinds of skills people need to work in jobs that involve a high degree of emotional labor. While the smile training, or charm school approaches, emphasized smiling at the customer, being nice, handling difficult customers tactfully, and giving the customer lots of strokes, the newer approach is toward helping the worker think independently, manage the moments of truth effectively, and acquire the skills necessary to handle an emotional-labor job without undue stress or fatigue.

Emotional-labor skills include some of the same skills such as building and maintaining rapport with the customer, handling difficult situations, and solving special customer problems. But in addition, employees learn techniques for keeping their stress levels down, keeping their physical energy up, not overreacting to abusive customers, and transacting with customers from a customer-first frame of reference.

In addition, with a service management philosophy, employees learn basic business and marketing facts. They learn about critical customer perceptions, the customer report card, and the critical attributes of the service customers consider most important. They also learn practical methods for analyzing their jobs and finding better ways to handle their moments of truth. The training encourages them to identify organizational systems and processes beyond their control that may be interfering with quality service and to bring them to management's attention along with suggestions for improving them.

Some organizations train their customer-contact employees separate from the internal-service employees, on the theory that each has special job needs and special skill needs. Others mix trainees from different kinds of jobs, different departments, and even different levels of rank, with the idea that they can all learn from each other and appreciate each others' needs more fully. Both approaches have merit. The method of choice will depend on the individual organization.

With a service management orientation, the training process attempts to make a salesperson out of every employee who comes into contact with the customer. We want each person to feel personally in charge of the moments of truth he or she deals with and committed to bringing the customer back for more. The training will succeed if a majority of the employees take the initiative in customer-first behavior and become committed to satisfying the customer instead of just doing a job.

FOLLOWING THROUGH ON TRAINING

One of the worst misuses of training as an organizational resource is simply training people with no follow-through. It is all too common in many companies, not only with respect to customer service training but with many other subjects as well. Training, all by itself, accomplishes relatively little. It can give people new ideas, new skills, and new attitudes. But it is not the primary determinant of the way they behave on the job. What determines how they behave on the job is the leadership they receive from their supervisors and the reinforcement signals they get from their work environment.

When the supervisors are not part of the planning and implementation process or if they are not fulfilling their roles as leaders and advocates of the service quality message, the employees get mixed signals. The trainer tells them how important it is to pay attention to the needs of their customers and to use a customer-first attitude all the time. But the supervisor tells them what to do, when to do it, and how to do it. If he or she nevers talks about the customer, or service, or quality, or pride, the message of the training fades.

Too many organizations just put their people through customer service training, with no preconditioning and no follow-through, and hope service will improve. It usually does, for a short period following the training. Then it usually sinks back to about the same level as before the training, because nobody is continuing to advocate customer service to them and make it crucially important on a daily basis.

Training in isolation can be an expensive waste of money at worst, and at best it cannot fully capitalize on the energy and enthusiasm it engenders in the employees. For a service quality program to work effectively, training must be part of an overall implementation with a concerted follow-through process to make it stick.

THE EFFECTS OF CULTURE AND LANGUAGE

Picture the following situation. A person is lying in a hospital bed, having just been admitted. In walks a person in a white uniform carrying a tray with some medicine on it. "What's that?" the patient enquires. The medications person, a Filipino, tries to explain, but her English is so limited that she can only smile helplessly and close the conversation with a nervous laugh. The patient is nervous too by this time. He says to himself, "This person can't speak English. How in the world can she communicate about things like medication, injections, and medical procedures?" The patient becomes at least mildly alarmed. He wonders whether he is receiving the right medication. Did she understand the doctor when he told her what to administer?

This situation repeats itself many times every day in hospitals around the country. Patients often can't tell who is who, and they tend to ask their questions of anybody who comes into their room. They believe anybody who comes into contact with them is a representative of the hospital and should be able to answer questions or get the answers. But hospitals depend heavily on low-paid workers, many of whom are immigrants. The lack of language skills on their part can be unnerving to people who, research shows, don't trust hospitals to begin with.

A less stressful, but still annoying situation occurs in food service many times. A person eating in a restaurant may signal the busboy to ask for an item the waitress forgot to bring. The busboy smiles, shrugs his shoulders embarrassedly, and says, "No English." It may be a small matter compared to the hospital situation, but it still detracts from the overall image of service. The customer feels that, if a person is going to work in a country where the primary language is English, he or she should learn to speak English, at least at a rudimentary level.

More and more organizations are dealing directly with the lack of language skills on the part of service workers. Some companies require a minimum competency in English as a condition for employment and grant a reasonable period of time for the employee to learn. Others even provide English as a second language (ESL) training on company time and at company expense. In industries and areas of the country where service workers are hard to recruit, they find it necessary to hire the ones that are available and make the investment to get them ready to function in public-contact jobs.

Roy Rogers Restaurants, a hamburger chain that is part of the Marriott family of companies, holds regular training sessions to teach service workers "Roy Rogers English," which consists of the basic vocabulary of food service and the Roy Rogers product line. It makes an important contribution to the customers' perceptions of service, and it contributes significantly to the personal lives of the workers.

Ethnic and cultural factors can have other effects on service quality besides language problems. A number of cruise lines, for example, operating out of Miami and serving the Bahamas draw from a labor market that includes a heavy concentration of East Indian workers, especially Haitians. Many of these people have not had the same social conditioning as the North Americans who are the customers. Many do not adhere to high personal standards of physical cleanliness and hygiene. When customers complain about body odor on the part of cabin attendants and restaurant servers, the ship's captain faces a delicate matter in getting adherence to standards.

Going back to the example of the patient who received the medication from the person who couldn't speak English well: this sometimes results in critical incidents that can endanger the patient. A number of American physicians who have worked with foreign-born nurses, especially Filipinos, believe the nurses are difficult to communicate with because of their culturally dictated deferential reactions toward people in authority such as physicians.

More than one doctor has told me, "I'm always a little bit uneasy when I give an instruction to one of these nurses. It may be a complicated procedure I'm telling her to carry out, and if she does it wrong the patient can be in big trouble. I'll ask her over and over again if she understands what I've just told her, and she'll smile shyly and nod her head. But I know damn well she's confused about it. She just won't speak up to me." What the doctor may consider an irresponsible attitude on the part of the nurse may really be an upside-down set of priorities dominated by a deeply-ingrained cultural rule.

Many Asian-born people are conditioned by their native cultures to avoid conflict and avoid being personally direct or assertive with others. These conditioning factors can become handicaps for them in English-speaking cultures where directness and clarity are much more highly valued than rapport and harmony.

Some of these cultural factors may also explain why public-contact service workers from certain ethnic backgrounds tend to be less cordial and outgoing to their customers. Most of the Asian cultures tend toward a social demeanor that is initially reserved, held back, unassertive, and even a bit passive. For people with this upbringing, it is offensive and presumptuous to climb all over a complete stranger and speak familiarly to him or her at the first instant of meeting, such as when the customer merely walks into a restaurant. While many Americans consider it normal and proper—except in the most "snooty" service environments—to be light and cordial in speaking to the customer, many Asians are horrified at the prospect.

I've often speculated that service people from some cultures may seem cold and impersonal not because they feel that way, but because they are acting according to other important values. In one recent incident, for example, I was dealing with a bellman of Asian extraction in a hotel in Honolulu. As I gave him my luggage, he made no greeting, didn't smile or recognize me in any way, and immediately turned his attention briskly to handling the cases. He gave me the claim checks and accepted the tip, again with no particular human signals. But when I asked him for a recommendation of a nearby restaurant where I could get a bowl of noodles for lunch, his demeanor changed instantly. He smiled warmly and gave me directions to his favorite noodle shop.

My conjecture about him, and possibly many others like him, was that the context of the interaction called for speed, efficiency, and service, not chit chat. The dominant value in the situation was to get the luggage handled quickly. He was a service person and was not on personal terms with the customer. For him, according to my theory, getting chummy with the customer at the first moment of contact would be a violation of role boundaries. But when I asked him about a relatively personal matter, he then had permission to expand the role definition and interact with me on a more personal basis. Thereafter, whenever I saw him in the hotel he gave me a wave and a pleasant smile.

The problem is that the values and expectations of the service person may not match those of the customers. We all know it is possible to insult or otherwise traumatize a person whose cultural background is very different from our own, just by doing the things we normally do. The issue in a service business becomes one of asking service people to adopt behaviors that are incongruent with their cultural programming.

This may not be as difficult as it first seems. If we assume most people are basically cordial and friendly under the right circumstances—i.e., right for their cultures—then it may be a matter of persuading them to see the moment of truth as the right circumstance. We need to help them understand that in European-derived cultures it's all right to be pleasant and cordial to strangers. We need to help them feel OK about expressing their view, or bringing problems to management attention, or even disagreeing with others without the disagreement being interpreted as conflict or disruptive to harmony. And we need to help them understand the importance of learning the language and customs of the country they're going to live in, so they can be more effective not only in their work lives but in their personal lives as well.

ORIENTING AND MANAGING
YOUNG WORKERS

Many service businesses operate with part-time jobs or with minimum-wage, unskilled jobs, and consequently they tend to draw on younger people for their staff. Fast-food businesses, restaurants, amusement parks, movie theaters, and supermarkets all tend to rely on teenagers to a large extent. Teenagers have the time flexibility to work in these kinds of businesses, and they will work for modest wages because they are just starting their working careers. Some supervisors in these kinds of businesses complain about the problems of working with kids, while others seem to get very good results. Young workers can be very productive and effective, but they need good leadership from their supervisors.

Most teenagers have certain natural assets for customer service jobs: they have boundless energy; they want to feel important and appreciated; they have a strong desire to please; and they tend to approach new jobs with fresh attitudes instead of becoming jaded as older workers may.

On the other hand, many teenagers have certain liabilities, which can present quite a challenge to those who have to supervise them: they tend to be immature and can't always control their energies; they are emotionally reactive, and get their feelings hurt or feel put down much more easily than they pretend; they are tremendously self-conscious and unsure of themselves; they need a lot of guidance and reassurance; they are very reactive to peer pressure and often lacking in self discipline; and they are inexperienced in their jobs and need a certain amount of teaching.

Although the list of liabilities is a bit longer than the assets, the possibilities are what count. By keeping certain things in mind, supervisors of young workers can give them the leadership and guidance they need to do an outstanding job of service.

Here are some simple rules supervisors need to follow in managing young workers:

1. Be realistic about their maturity levels. Recognize that they are in a growing-up process. They may try to act worldly and sophisticated, but they are not nearly as mature and self-reliant as they pretend.

2. Be willing to teach and develop them. You can't expect them to know the same things or have the same level of experience as older workers. You'll need to give them a lot of help, attention, and guidance at first.

3. Make your expectations very clear and unequivocal when they first come to work. Set high standards for customer-first behavior and let them know their jobs depend on their doing things right by the customers.

4. Talk to them in plain, down-to-earth language. Make your pep talks or tutorial sessions very short, simple, and to the point. Don't overestimate their capacity for abstract conceptualization, and don't overtax their attention span with long meetings and elaborate explanations.

5. Give them frequent guidance and encouragement. They need lots of affirmation of their work and they need to feel appreciated. Be very sparing with criticism or fault finding.

6. Expect the best from every one of them. Don't accept inferior work, inattentiveness to their jobs, horseplay, impoliteness to the customers, unreliable work attendance, or any other immature behavior. They will come up to whatever standard you set for them.

CORPORATE COMMUNICATION PROGRAMS

Training is really just one part of the overall communication process that must go on in the organization if the message of service quality is to reach and affect everyone working there. There needs to be a broad, all-encompassing effort to raise the collective awareness of service, of the customer's needs, and of cooperation and teamwork in the name of quality.

Three groups of people, or audiences, need to receive a constant message about service quality and their parts in it: the executives, the middle managers, and the frontline people, including frontline supervisors.

In a top-down service quality program, the executives must be the most aware, most enlightened, and most committed of all. It is up to them to communicate the message down through their areas of the organization, so they must fully understand it and believe in it. There should be plenty of attention given at the outset to getting the service strategy and the service philosophy clear in the minds of all the top leaders. They must speak with a common voice to the rest of the organization, so they must all share the same gospel. Executive retreats, occasional executive conferences devoted to the status of the service program, and occasional problem-solving meetings will keep the subject uppermost in their minds.

The middle managers represent a special population, in need of a special communication process. In many organizations, the middle managers get left out of the process. Top management launches a big service quality program, puts on the employee training programs, sets up the task forces, and everybody gets down to work while the middle managers sit around and watch. They are often disenfranchised from their roles as leaders and made into functionaries who merely apply policies and interpret rules. If they are left out of the communication process that launches the program, and if they are not a fundamental part of the implementation process, it isn't reasonable to expect them to give their wholehearted support to it or to preach and teach it to their employees.

Your middle managers deserve the benefit of an intensive, focused development process suited to their needs as potential leaders and advocates in the service program. It makes sense to begin with them before taking the training programs to the front line. You need to get all, or at least most, of your middle managers involved, up to speed, committed, and thinking about how they will implement the program in their areas. This can be done through one or more training seminars, meetings with top management to go over the program objectives, and planning workshops in which they work together to develop implementation plans. As the program rolls along, there should be frequent review meetings and continued planning sessions to help them stay on top of the implementation process and feel a sense of ownership in it.

Finally, the frontline people need to hear about the service program more than once. If they attend the training sessions and then never hear about service again, they will assume it was just a one-time pep talk. The message of quality service needs to be so completely present in their working environment, so dominant in the day-to-day thinking process, that they simply cannot avoid seeing and hearing it. The communication campaign can consist of a number of options beyond the initial training sessions:

1. Follow-up training sessions dealing with specific service issues and topics; showing of educational films on various aspects of service jobs.
2. Occasional program rallies that report progress and reinforce the service message.
3. Meetings with their supervisors and middle managers to renew the commitment to quality service and to discuss the obstacles that interfere with service.
4. Regular, periodic newsletters that highlight excellent service performance on the part of various employees and give progress reports on how the organization is improving service.
5. Corporate video programs, i.e., video newsletters, either over closed-circuit television or distributed to field units for local showing.
6. Working level paraphernalia—used tastefully, please—that serve as reminders of service quality; these can include posters in work areas, notepads with service quality reminders printed on them, and unobtrusive stickers at key places that call attention to key customer-pleasing actions. Go easy with lapel buttons with service slogans on them; make sure the job aids fit comfortably with the employees' conception of dealing with their customers.
7. The occasional Big Event, i.e., a gathering or celebration that focuses on service quality; this can include the regular annual management meeting, an occasional all-hands gath-

ering to recognize the employees who give outstanding service, and kickoff events that ceremonialize new aspects of the service package such as new products or new ways of delivering the service.

In addition to all of these specific elements of corporate communication, many other things communicate. As we shall discuss in a later chapter, the day-to-day behavior of managers, at all levels, communicates clearly to employees. If the managers think, talk, and act service quality, so will the workers. When employees see their peers getting recognized publicly and rewarded for excellent service work, they get the message quickly. The number one means for communicating service excellence is management's action.

CHAPTER 13

PHASE 4: IMPLEMENT GRASS-ROOTS IMPROVEMENTS

Take care of the means and the end will take care of itself.
—*Gandhi*

PLANT MANY SEEDS

The fourth phase of the model service quality program is implementation of grass-roots improvements in the way the organization produces and delivers its service products. During this phase, we hope for a transfer of ownership in the program. What began as a top-down initiative must transform itself into a movement at the work-unit level that has energy and life of its own. We hope the idea of service quality and the strategy for service will be sufficiently attractive and compelling that the employees and their supervisors will take it to themselves, put it to use in their jobs, and turn it into whatever they need to make their moments of truth the best they can be.

It's not enough for top management to believe in and advocate the program. Middle management support, while critical, is also not enough. We must try to plant many seeds, all around the organization, if we are going to get the whole thing to grow and flower.

In the fourth phase of the ideal service quality program, things begin to happen spontaneously at the unit levels and even at the level of the frontline employees, among both customer-contact employees and internal-service employees. People begin to pay more attention to the customer; they begin to exhibit customer-first behavior more extensively and consistently; they begin to make demands on their leaders, in terms of the support and assistance they need to manage their moments of truth effectively; and they begin to question and challenge organizational rules and systems that stand in the way of service excellence.

In a sense, we are trying to foster a kind of constructive subversiveness, i.e., a certain attitude on the part of the working people and their leaders, that demands a lot of the organization. We want them to believe in the idea of service so much that they become the advocates of service quality in the organization. Rather than wait for someone to come along and tell them how to improve service, they need to light their own candles, wherever they are, and make the best contribution they can.

The methods described in this chapter can all contribute to this process of transferring of ownership and making the employees the advocates of quality service.

THE SERVICE QUALITY TASK FORCE

I have mentioned several times that I advocate the task-force approach in making major changes in organizations. In fact, I consider a service quality task force as virtually essential to get the program well underway and maintain its momentum. A service quality venture can quickly grind to a halt if it doesn't have the benefit of one or more people who keep pushing it along, day after day, week after week, month after month.

A task force can serve this role very effectively if:

1. It has the right members. It needs to include people with organizational clout as well as people who know the various operations and appreciate the service problems. All of them have to have the energy, commitment, enthusiasm, and willingness to work together to make the task force a strong agent of change.
2. It has a strong leader—someone the others respect and are willing to take direction from; someone who knows how to pull people together and get them to function as a team; someone who has the maturity and communication skills to get the best contribution each person has to offer.
3. It has a clear mission to accomplish and a clear understanding of its entitlement to act.

4. It has a clear mandate from the chief executive officer to carry out its business. It must have access to senior executives whenever needed, and it must feel the effects of their expectations of results.
5. It has a clear, simple, realistic plan and timetable for implementing the program.
6. It has access to resources in the organization that may be needed in implementing particular tasks, projects, or changes. It needs to have access to money, people, talent, management direction, and information.

The proper number of members on the task force varies according to the needs of the program, but it should stay at a convenient size. With less than six, it's hard to maintain energy and momentum. With more than 15 or so, it becomes a bit of a mob. If you have that many people interested and committed, consider subdividing the task force into major committees, with a few people from each committee attending the overall task force meetings. A convenient number of members is about 10.

It's also a good idea to include people with a wide range of perspectives on the task force. It usually makes sense to include frontline employees in addition to people from specialty areas and some managers. A vice president or two also helps, especially when the task force needs somebody with some clout to clear obstacles out of the way.

If the task force is well-appointed, well-chartered, and well-led, it can serve a number of important roles in carrying out the service quality program. It can perform at least the following functions:

1. Handle the program executive function; guide the overall program along its schedule, review and report progress, monitor resources, and manage consulting efforts.
2. Hook people and groups together to help them attack service problems that span more than one unit's territory.
3. Take specific initiatives to study selected service problems and recommend solutions to management.
4. Help others set up subcommittees or subprojects that can attack specific problems and bring the results back to the task force for consideration.

5. Reinforce training activities by following through with various small-unit activities planned and directed from the task-force level.
6. Manage the corporate communication process that carries the service message to all parts of the organization; publicize the results of the program, give special recognition to people who deserve it, and keep the idea of service quality uppermost in people's minds.

The people on the service quality task force need to have the time and energy to devote to their mission. It won't work if they just hold an occasional meeting on a sporadic basis, with half the membership present. They must be an action group, and they must be willing and able to give it the proper commitment of energy. The task force will be very active in the earliest phases of the program. The members might find it necessary and worthwhile to meet at least once a week at first. As things get underway, they may meet less often, say, every other week for a while, and then perhaps every month as the program is well along.

It is also important that every member of the task force be active and reliable. If a person can't attend most of the meetings or fades out of contact for a long period, it is fair for the task force leader to ask that person to relinquish his or her membership to someone who can fulfill the commitment.

Occasionally the task force should review and analyze its own activities and modes of operation to see whether it is making as strong a contribution to the success of the program as it can.

MIDDLE MANAGEMENT LEADERSHIP

In too many organizations, middle management operates like an inertial resistance factor in the face of new initiatives launched from the top. I've often heard executives complaining as they look back on two or three years of experience with a companywide program of some sort, saying, "I wish we had gotten middle management on board with us. Somehow they never really gave it their support."

If you don't want to be singing that song two or three years into the program, it makes sense to build the program in such a way that middle managers can play an essential part in moving it into the organization. Senior management needs to make very clear to middle managers the part they will play in the program's success. Each middle manager should be expected to examine his or her own operation with respect to the overall organizational service initiative and to determine how the department will carry it out. Each one needs to have a clear, concise, and realistic written plan for implementing quality service within his or her area.

The plan should include, as a minimum:

1. A clear statement of the department's service mission, whether it is external service to the paying customer, internal service to the organizational customer, or a combination of both.
2. A clear identification of the department's customer population and a report card that defines service quality as perceived by those customers.
3. A set of steps the manager will take to preach, teach, and reinforce the philosophy of service and to reinforce the messages presented in the training sessions.
4. An overall plan for improving the department's service product in a systematic way, with specific objectives, actions, and timetables.

Top management needs to lay the responsibility for service improvement squarely in the hands of the middle managers and expect them to follow through. The task force can look after those matters that affect the organization overall, but individual managers must ultimately make the service program come alive in their units and keep it going by the strength of their leadership.

APPLICATION LABS

One of the most effective ways to carry the service quality training over to the job situation is to use a type of on-the-job training method called an application lab. This is an informal, small-group teaching activity that zeroes in on some specific aspect of the group's service work. In a typical application lab, a trainer from the human resources development department visits a particular work group—by invitation—and spends from an hour to two hours with the group. The meeting is usually about half training and half problem solving.

The trainer discusses the group's service mission with group members, and they identify an aspect of the operation they would like to improve. It could be a procedure or a system problem they want to deal with, or it could be an area where they would like more skill building than the training program provided. The trainer guides the group process, using some of the service management tools such as the customer report card or the cycle of service model, to help them think through the problem. As they work through the process, the group members gain two benefits: they get a solution to the problem, and they learn to use the problem-solving process. Thereafter, they can use the process on their own, without the consultant.

By conducting application labs all over the organization, the HRD department can immediately extend the effect of the main training program and make sure it doesn't begin to fade. Ideally, this process becomes self-reinforcing as various work units use it to pinpoint and solve problems that stand in the way of service quality. This again is the process of planting many seeds all around the organization.

SERVICE CIRCLES

Another very effective technique, similar to the application lab but more permanent, is the *service circle* approach. A service circle is very similar to the quality circle approach, except it focuses on service quality issues and it uses the tools of service management rather than the traditional manufacturing-oriented quality analysis methods.

A service circle is a group of employees, usually within a single work unit working with their supervisor, who meet on a regular basis to identify and solve service problems or to invent ways to improve service. This method is another powerful way to get frontline people involved and to put them in charge of finding solutions.

British Airways has made effective use of the service circle approach with a program they refer to as customer-first teams. More than 100 customer-first teams at BA facilities all over the world have contributed several thousand specific, operational improvements. One example of a service circle idea that led to an important marketing and operational innovation concerned the company's handling of unaccompanied children as passengers.

A customer-first team was meeting to identify additional opportunities for service improvement, when someone mentioned the problem of unaccompanied minors. Minors traveling alone represent a liability for the airline, and the flight crews have to be especially alert to keep them in care and custody all the time until they meet someone at their destination. During the discussion, one BA employee asked, "Why do we call them 'unaccompanied minors'? Sounds like we're programming ourselves—and them—to think about them as problems rather than as customers." This led to a discussion of ways to make the flying experience better for children.

As a result of the discussion, the group recommended changing the designation from "unaccompanied minor" to "young flyer." The change turned out to be much more than superficial, because it led to development of a Young Flyer's Program. The group worked out special activities for young flyers, including a preflight briefing in a special corner of the waiting lounge; a special young flyer's ticket envelope and boarding pass, both of which could become souvenirs after the flight; special meals; and special treatment on-board, including a visit to the flight deck and briefing by the pilot.

This is typical of the kind of imaginative solutions frontline service people can come up with if given the freedom to think originally and look for new and better ways to do the job. Upper managers are much less likely to think up approaches like this, because they are much further from the customer than the frontline people.

Similarly, Santa Monica Hospital staffers formed a service circle to study the patient-admissions process. They decided to eliminate the "forms-first" syndrome so characteristic of healthcare facilities. They set up customer-first rules for greeting the patient, making him or her feel comfortable and welcome, and then working in the paperwork as part of the process, not as the apparent top priority.

Another service circle, formed by a group of nurses, redesigned the discharge procedure and prepared a handy checklist for the patient and family to eliminate the typical delays that had plagued the process. They streamlined the method for getting prescriptions handled by the hospital pharmacy, so patients would be spared the wait at the pharmacy counter on their way out of the hospital.

To work effectively, a service circle needs three things:

1. A skillful leader or a trained consultant or facilitator to work with the circle.
2. A strong sense of team spirit.
3. Some basic skills and methods in creative problem solving.

Organizations that set up extensive service circle programs usually put the circle leaders through skill training in creative problem-solving techniques as part of the preparation. They often train roving group facilitators as well, much like the application lab trainers, who can go from group to group and help them work through their local issues.

To get the process started, begin with those unit supervisors who show the most determination and imagination about improving the levels of service their groups provide. The trained facilitators can help these groups come up with worthwhile results that can draw the attention and appreciation of the other groups. It is generally best to make participation voluntary at the outset, rather than ordering supervisors to form service circles. Each supervisor has his or her own way of improving service, and requiring everybody to use the same approach usually causes a backlash.

It is probable, however, that some supervisors may be less enthusiastic and supportive of the objectives of the service quality program than management would like. It is fair, in my view, for management to expect a reasonable effort at self-assessment and planned service improvement. If a supervisor is behaving completely passively, management's job is to make it clear that service quality is the objective and that action is in order. Setting up a service circle in such a unit may be a comfortable way for the supervisor to respond to management urging, before the urging takes the form of direct pressure to get the job done.

It is a good idea, once the service circles are underway, to report on their progress frequently and to hold occasional meetings of the circle leaders. This way they can trade ideas, learn from one another, and encourage one another.

THE T-CHART

One of the most useful service management tools, and one that can make every customer-contact employee more effective, is the T-chart. The T-chart is a very simple job aid that enables the employee to analyze his or her service job and find ways to personalize it and make it more human in dealing with the customer. It is especially effective in making employees who have become robotized in their jobs aware of that fact and in showing them how to put warmth and concern back into the way they handle each moment of truth.

To use the T-chart model, the employee simply draws a T-shaped diagram on a sheet of paper, with two columns, as in Figure 13–1. On the left column of the chart, the employee lists the specific *task actions* involved in the moment of truth, which might be receiving the customer's payment at the cash register, answering a telephone request, filling out a form with the customer, administering a medication, taking an order for a meal, handling a banking transaction, or any other task of a similar magnitude. These are the mechanical, nonpersonal parts of the moment of truth.

On the right side of the T-chart, the employee lists specific *personal actions*—things he or she can say or do that make the customer feel at ease, comfortable, appreciated, and special. These might include a smile, a friendly greeting, a touch if appropriate, a little joke, or some polite conversation. All of these can

FIGURE 13–1
The T-Chart Helps to De-Robotize the Job

The T–Chart	
My Moment of Truth: _____	
Task Actions	*Personal Actions*
1. I explain procedures	1. Greet customer
2. We fill out form	2. Make conversation
3. Customer reviews	3. Use humor
4. Customer approves	4. Etc.
5. Etc.	5. Etc.

add a personal touch to the moment of truth and take it out of the realm of the impersonal, mechanized transactions that make up so much of the mediocre service people complain about.

The T-chart has a place in the basic training of service quality. Introducing it during the training sessions sets the stage for its use by virtually all employees. It is good material for application labs. Service circles can use it as a learning model for analyzing the work of the unit. Supervisors can meet with each of their employees and help them diagram their jobs using the T-chart.

And when a supervisor sees that a particular frontline service employee is turning into a robot, he or she can sit down with that person and use the T-chart to explain the problem and show the person how to become less robotic and more natural.

REDESIGNING SERVICE SYSTEMS

Systems are often the enemies of service for two reasons. First, many of them have never been consciously designed by anybody. Like Topsy, they just grew. Over the years, the various units in an organization work out their methods, rules, procedures, protocols, and information tools by evolution. Often, they make little sense to the people who have to use them. It is common for procedural systems to include processes that have become obsolete, but that everyone still follows because nobody thinks they can be changed.

The second reason systems often work against service is that, even when they have been consciously designed, the design seldom starts with the premise of maximizing service quality. Customer handling systems, customer record keeping systems, data processing systems, accounting systems, and reporting systems usually grow from the desires of various departments to make their own work easier. Seldom do they look at the designs of these systems with a view toward maximizing customer convenience or customer satisfaction.

Case in Point: I walked into a bank one morning to take care of what I considered a small matter. I had a checking account at the bank, which I had not used for some time because I had transferred my checking to another bank. I also had a credit card account through this bank, with a balance owing. The checking account balance was somewhat more than the credit card balance, so I thought I would use the checking funds to pay off the credit card. I had lost the checkbook sometime ago, so I knew I would have to write a counter check to transfer the funds.

I went into the bank shortly after it opened. I got into the main waiting line—i.e., the line you wait in to find out what line you're supposed to be in—and when my turn came I explained what I wanted to do. The young lady I talked with could not complete the transaction for me; she could only give the figures for the balances of the two accounts. She sent me to the other end of the counter to wait in line to speak to the woman who could prepare the counter check. When my turn came again, she prepared the counter check, but refused to take the check in payment of the credit card account.

She said, "I'm not a teller. You'll have to get in line and give the check to a teller." I said, "I don't understand. You work for the bank; the teller works for the bank. Why can't you just take this check and give it to the person who is supposed to get it? Why should I wait in three lines just to take care of such a small matter?"

She gave me that stone-cold, passive expression I've come to recognize in people who have been fully robotized by the systems they work for and said again, "I'm sorry; I'm not a teller. You'll have to get in line and give it to a teller."

Ignoring the lessons of experience, I—a disgruntled customer—decided to tangle with this insane service "system." I asked to speak to someone in authority. A woman came over who seemed to be a supervisor of something. I explained my request to her and she said, "I'm sorry, you'll have to get in line and give it to a teller."

Here was a case of system craziness. This organization had systematized itself into service mediocrity. I'm sure the counter clerk felt like a nitwit, having to tell her customer she wasn't authorized to think. And I suppose the supervisor had a fleeting moment of recognition of the absurdity of the situation. Because their system only allowed a certain person at a certain station to hit the check with the rubber stamp, and they were not authorized to complete the communication process themselves, they had no choice but to give the customer the runaround.

I was tired of waiting in lines, especially because the bank lobby was filling up with customers and the lines were getting longer and longer. So I went back to my office and mailed the check. I'm sure it cost them more to accept the check that way than if they had merely accepted it over the counter, but nobody disobeyed the rules.

One of the first things to be done in any major service quality program is to look at the design of the systems that affect the customer's perception of service, either directly or indirectly. Consider every customer-impact system guilty unless proven innocent.

A *customer-impact system* is any organizational structure, procedure, method, or rule that causes a result the customer can perceive. Some customer-impact systems work beautifully on behalf of the customer and create positive impressions of service. Others may cause the customer inconvenience, extra effort, frustration, or concern about the service. We want all customer-impact systems to be designed with service quality in mind. Here are some of the most obvious customer-impact systems to look at in your organization.

Organizational Structures.   Sometimes the arrangement of the blocks on the organization chart forces the customer to deal with you in an unnatural or inconvenient way. Too narrow and too strict a departmentalization of effort leads to a compartmentalization of service. The customer has to climb up one ladder to deal with one set of monkeys perched there and then climb back down and go climb up another ladder to deal with another set of monkeys. The separate ladders keep the monkeys from communicating with one another, so the customer is the one who has to complete the circuit.

Data Systems.   It's amazing how often data processing people have to say, "Sorry—the computer system isn't set up to do that. We can't do it that way." In many banks, for example, the data systems have grown like a patch of weeds, with no customer orientation about their design. You'd be surprised how many bank marketing managers can't get a simple report on a single customer showing the various financial activities that customer has with the bank. The checking account system is separate from the certificate-of-deposit system, which is separate from the loan system, which is separate from the home-mortgage system, which is separate from the line-of-credit sales system. All of the subsystems were developed independently, with no common customer data base. For each new action, the customer has to fill out the same information again on a new form. In some banks, the only way to find out everything the customer has with the bank is to ask the customer.

Customer Information Media.   Many of the documents service organizations push at their customers can barely be understood by lawyers, let alone the customers. Insurance policies, individual retirement account documents, loan agreements, medical plans, and real estate paperwork can be incomprehensible. The typical bank's loan agreement is written by the wrong people, i.e., the lawyers rather than the salespeople. The formidable document starts by establishing, at least by implication, that the customer is probably a crook and is not to be trusted. The harsh legal terminology and implied threats of legal action if the customer violates any of the bank's rules are enough to turn anybody off. There is no hint of performing a service or of acting as a partner in the success of the person borrowing the money. The preoccupation of the document is with making sure the customer doesn't try to cheat the bank. More and more banks are experimenting with "plain English" loan agreements and other customer documents, but the trend is moving more slowly than it should.

Customer Rules.   Any time you impose a rule on your customer, you'd better be prepared for a negative impression of your service quality. It does little good to put up the sign that says, *"To serve you better,* we require three forms of identification in order to cash your check." Who's kidding whom? How can anybody in his or her right mind conclude this is for the purpose of serving the customer better? At least let's not insult the customer's intelligence.

Serial Procedures.   A serial procedure is one in which one department after another handles the customer's problem, with each one adding its own contribution to the total time it takes to get the job done. In many organizations, the various departments work at their own convenience rather than at the convenience of the customer. Each one says, "I can't do anything with it until Department X gets through with it." So the process takes weeks or months as it wends its way through the bureaucratic peristalsis. Serial procedures are often good candidates for service improvement. With a little imagination and common sense, it is often possible to streamline them and speed them up. You may find that improving the service quality this way also cuts costs by eliminating unnecessary steps.

Interdepartmental Handoffs.   Some service processes require a great deal of coordination among departments or work units. Every time there is a handoff, i.e., a change of responsibility from one department to another, there is a chance for a mistake that can make a negative impression on the customer.

Cycles of Service.   A cycle of service is a complete sequence of events the customer experiences in getting his or her needs met. It starts with the first moment of truth and continues through a series of related moments of truth until the customer is satisfied with the result and is willing to come back and partake of the service again. Looking at a service in terms of a cycle of service is really looking at it from the customer's point of view, not the organization's. The customer doesn't care about your departments or internal territories. The only thing that matters to the customer is getting his or her needs met. Analyzing and streamlining cycles of service is an excellent way to get people thinking in customer-first terms.

If senior management really wants to go down the road of service quality and service commitment, it will be necessary to take a close and critical look at all the customer-impact systems in the organization. Some of them may be near and dear to the hearts of various department managers with vested interests in doing things the current way. But sometimes it becomes necessary to turn certain sacred cows out to pasture and get on with the process of modernization and refocusing resources and energy away from self-serving interests and toward service quality.

CHAPTER 14

PHASE 5: MAKE IT PERMANENT

> What you stroke is what you get.
> —*Eric Berne*
> *Creator of transactional analysis*

The ultimate objective of a service quality program is to disappear—to stop being a program and just become part of the woodwork. The program needs eventually to dissolve into the background of the organization so its boundaries are no longer distinguishable from the day-to-day business. It has to become part of "the way we do things around here."

This process of becoming permanent may take some time. It is realistic to think in terms of two to three years before the service commitment is firmly in place and playing a primary part in the thinking process of the organization's managers and frontline employees.

The fifth phase of our model service quality program, making it permanent, can start on day one. There is no reason to conceive of the five basic phases in this model as strictly separated in time, with no overlap. Indeed, they can and should overlap and each phase should get underway as soon as the conditions are ready for it.

Here are some thoughts on how to help the process become permanent, and how to recognize the signs that it is becoming so.

THE EVERYDAY SIGNS TELL THE TALE

You can tell whether an organization is customer oriented by looking at everyday things. All you have to do is look and listen as people go about their business. People talk service routinely, not deliberately or self-consciously. You hear them talking about the service quality, about customer satisfaction, about recovery when things go wrong, and about adding value to the customer's experience. The customer focus is a basic part of the way they conceive of what they do. They pay attention to the details of the customer interface. They keep an eye on the critical moments of truth and act to assure quality in them. They test every little change or new way of doing things against the criteria of customer impact.

In most highly service-oriented businesses, there is a tactical orientation in the way managers act. They may do a lot of strategic thinking and high-level meeting, but they also have a personal feel for the service product and the way it is delivered to customers. In a world-class restaurant or hotel, the manager doesn't sit hidden away in a plush office and go over the financial reports. He or she is out and around, interacting with customers and employees. In a world-class hotel or restaurant *chain,* the executives are out catering to the employees at the local operations because they are the customers. The executives in customer-driven businesses always seem to have their eye on what's happening with both the paying customers and the internal, working customers.

Returning to the service triangle, the basic model of service management, we recall the three broad characteristics of excellent service businesses:

1. A vision, or strategy, for service.
2. Customer-oriented frontline people.
3. Customer-friendly systems.

The vision, the people, and the systems must work together to make the promise of service quality come true for the customer. When all of the parts are in place and working, you can see it, you can hear it, and you can feel it.

DO THE MANAGERS WALK THEIR TALK?

In a service-oriented business, the behavior of the managers is congruent with the service strategy. They act to implement the basic service concept and commitment set forth by senior management as a result of the market research. If the key factor in customer satisfaction is minimizing the waiting time, say in a bank, the managers talk to people about waiting time and about new and better ways to reduce or control it. If the key factor is accuracy, say in a hospital ward, the managers talk to people about accuracy of medications, medical records, patient information, and meal menus delivered to bedsides.

If customer satisfaction depends heavily on a personal touch, such as in hospitality or food service, the managers pull people's attention to the personal touch. They let employees know if they are turning into robots and remind them to treat each customer like somebody special. If it is speed of order processing, as in a mail-order business, they talk to people about speed—about order turnaround, speed of shipping, speed of issuing refunds, speed of answering the telephone. Whatever counts is what they harp on, all the time.

It doesn't take long for a manager to get the point across if he or she keeps the focus on the key idea of service—whatever it is that makes a hit with the customer. People begin to understand by second nature that the name of the game is customer satisfaction, and they know what they have to do to achieve and maintain it.

Another key element of the everyday landscape of the service business, to be discussed in more depth later, is the measurement process. In the minds of the employees:

It's not what you *expect*, but what you *inspect* that counts.

Whatever the boss seems to pay attention to, measure, evaluate, and report to upper management tends to become the unconscious priority of workers. If it's compliance with rules, you get compliance with rules. If it's not spending money, you get not spending money. If it's service quality, you get service quality. It's that simple.

In the words of J. Willard Marriott, Jr., head of the Marriott Corporation, "You have to live it."

THE SYSTEMS MUST SUPPORT THE SERVICE

Systems can be the enemies of service, and we should make system design and function subordinate to the overall driving idea of service quality.

You can't expect people to strive for excellence with mediocre tools.

The previous chapter described a means of attack on organizational systems that impede service. For the present discussion, remember the service ethic can never be permanent in the organization as long as "system craziness" still exists. Systems that don't work or don't make sense will always present obstacles to making service the best it can be. An important part of getting to the fifth stage of making it permanent is facing up to and fixing systems that need it.

EMPLOYEE SELECTION AND HIRING: CAN YOU BOTTLE ATTITUDE?

Building a service-oriented work force is a long-term goal of service development. Although people at work respond to the environment around them and to the direction they get from their supervisors, it helps to rig the game for success at the outset by getting people into service jobs that are well suited for the work. This means selecting people carefully and then orienting them properly before they ever begin work.

Employee selection has been a confusing problem for managers in service businesses because it is usually difficult to define the knowledge, attitudes, skills, and habits necessary to succeed in service work. Customer-contact jobs involve an element of emotional labor as described in a previous chapter. Emotional labor is hard to define, and the competency for it is hard to measure. It is one thing to measure physical strength, manual dexterity, technical knowledge, or typing speed. It is another matter to try to measure warmth, concern for customers, interpersonal skills, and emotional resiliency. Yet that is what we must eventually learn to do if we are going to get service-oriented people into service jobs.

American organizations have also been handicapped by misinterpreted civil rights laws that make many personnel officers fearful about using employee tests of almost any kind. The landmark Supreme Court case of *Griggs* v. *Duke Power* struck down virtually all pencil-and-paper tests used for employee hiring and promotion unless they can be shown to be operationally valid for the specific job skills under consideration.

In the Griggs case, a yard worker who was black was denied promotion to the job of sweeper because he could not pass a written examination. The Supreme Court ruled the company, Duke Power, had discriminated against him in its practices because it could not show that a person needed to be able to read or write in order to operate a broom. As a result of this case, the vast majority of American corporations dropped almost all forms of written tests in order to defend themselves against accusations of racial or ethnic discrimination.

A number of companies have tried to develop job-valid screening tests for employee selection, but so far no test has found its way into wide use. This area still needs attention and represents a major opportunity if a fair and valid instrument can be developed. One such attempt is the Work Attitude Scale, developed by an Australian firm. It is a simple questionnaire given to the person who is applying for a customer service job. The applicant answers a short series of yes or no questions. The computer scoring procedure develops two measurement factors: people orientation and task orientation.

The rationale for the screening is that workers with a high people orientation are more likely to adapt successfully to the interpersonal demands of customer-contact work without becoming overly stressed by contact overload. Those with a high task orientation and low people orientation would be better off in task-oriented jobs with little or no repetitive customer contact.

In studies with supermarket cashiers, for instance, the Work Attitude Scale indicated a fairly sharp cutoff score, above which employees tended to succeed well in the cashiering job and below which they tended to have difficulty or even flunk out. Retrospectively, it was concluded that hiring only employees whose scores on the test exceeded the cutoff point would have increased the job-success rate from about 50 percent to about 80 percent. The study methodology defined job failure as either getting fired for cause or leaving the company in a no-rehire status.

Any screening device used in the United States would have to be anonymous in its application. That is, the manager evaluating the candidates would have to have no knowledge about the race, color, age, sex, religion, or national origin of any applicant. The screening test could be used only to narrow the original supply of applicants for final interviews, not to make firm hiring decisions.

Another important aspect of personnel policy is to help people out of jobs in which they are not successful. If, in the manager's judgment, a person is not suited for a public-contact job, it makes sense to move that person into another line of work in which he or she can make a worthwhile contribution. It makes no sense to leave a person in such a job, because there will be a negative impact on the person as well as the customer. It is the manager's responsibility to keep only the best-qualified people at the customer interface and not to tolerate work attitudes or behavior that detract from the service image.

Another very important element in building and maintaining a service culture is the employee orientation process. This is a huge missed opportunity in many organizations, some of which have no employee orientation process at all. Consider the significance of a new employee's entry into the organizational culture the first day, the first week, the first month of employment. During this critical period, the new person reads the corporate environment, sees what other people do, hears how they talk and finds out what they think, and begins to form the basis for his or her own work attitudes and habits that will probably continue for a long time. Why leave this crucial process of perception and attitude formation to chance?

Most of the leading service organizations provide their new employees with intensive orientation programs soon after they arrive. These programs play a key role in indoctrinating them in the service philosophy, customer-first attitudes, and service methods that make the organizations outstanding.

At Disneyland, for instance, new employees don't go near their jobs until they have completed a basic one-day class in what it means to be a Disney employee. In "Traditions 1," they learn who Walt Disney was, what he believed in, and what his philosophy was about entertainment. They learn they are in the entertainment industry, not the amusement-park industry. Their product is fun and fantasy in a show-business atmosphere, so they have to learn how to think and act like show-business people.

Disney employees are expected to know a lot about the Disney product line, i.e., the beloved Walt Disney characters and the fictional personalities the various park attractions portray. The sweepers and cleaners learn that they will be the people whom the customers most often seek out with questions about the park. They are expected to know the answers by heart.

By the time the new employee goes into the job, he or she already has a basic mind-set about what the Disneyland experience should be for the customer and what it means to work there and be part of the experience. In both Anaheim and Orlando, the Disney parks draw the cream of the crop among young workers, and most of the other service businesses in their areas have to work hard to attract the kinds of kids they want to hire.

Quality begets quality, and the kind of quality orientation instilled in the new Disney worker leads to a stronger and more durable commitment to quality later. That leads to a sense of pride in being associated with a quality product, which affects the others who apply for jobs with Disney. The process feeds on itself. Whereas mediocrity in service causes a vicious cycle leading to more mediocrity, excellence in service causes a virtuous cycle leading to a continued commitment to excellence. Getting there is a tough battle; staying there is more a matter of keeping the focus.

MEASUREMENT AND FEEDBACK

I believe every service organization needs to have a service quality measurement system that tells executives, managers, and employees how the service team is performing in the eyes of the customers. Frontline people need to know how they are doing in their jobs and whether their efforts on behalf of the customer are paying off. Supervisors need to know how well their units are contributing to the overall service image of the company. Middle managers need to assess the support and assistance they are giving to the line units and to learn what improvements they can make. And executives need to know how well the whole organization is working and to what extent service quality is making a difference in the marketplace.

The service quality measurement system, or SQMS, should produce a report or a series of reports that tell these various interest groups what they need to know to do their jobs well. The basis for SQMS can usually be the customer report card, as discussed previously. The customer report card resulted from the customer perception research that told us what key attributes of the service product the customers consider important. If you have a useful customer report card, all that remains to have an SQMS is to convert the various service attributes into measured variables, set up a means for gathering data from the customers, set up a means for processing the data, and create a format for presenting the results in understandable form.

The quickest way to visualize an SQMS for your organization is to look at a typical live system. Santa Monica Hospital set up a three-part measurement system to assess the perceptions of physicians—traditionally considered the "real" customers of the hospital—the patients, and the staff. Management wanted inputs from all three interest groups for a composite picture of service quality.

We started with the customer report cards that emerged from the market research. Attributes important to doctors were identified on one report card, and attributes important to their patients on another report card. A third report card was synthesized for employees based on perceptions of service they reported in an organizational climate survey that also dealt with attitudes about service quality. With these three report cards representing the key attributes of judgment on the part of the three constituent populations, we created three corresponding questionnaires, one for each group.

The patient questionnaire has two versions, one for in-patients and one for out-patients, since their experiences with hospital services are usually significantly different. With all three questionnaires, we use a standard 5-point rating scale, with 1 representing a low score and 5 representing a high score. This scheme makes it easy for managers and employees to read and quickly interpret the statistical reports; by knowing that a high score is a good score, one can quickly browse through the 50 or so questions and spot the strong areas and the areas that need attention.

All questionnaire responses are anonymous. All patients and their doctors receive questionnaires at the time of the patient's discharge, along with postage-paid reply envelopes. They are processed and reported on a monthly basis.

According to Angie Twarynski, hospital coordinator for the service quality program and head of the task force, "With the service quality measurement system, we can tell at a glance how we're scoring with our customers—the doctors and their patients. We also get the perceptions of our staff on factors like organizational service image, their personal levels of morale and commitment, and their perceptions of management's commitment to service quality. Using our personal-computer software program, we can look at various subpopulations in the data such as specific physician specialties, or patients in certain age ranges, or male-female differences. We now have a snapshot of our service quality which we never had before."

Your own SQMS will reflect your organization's customer characteristics and the key attributes of your own service. You will have to tailor a system to fit your own needs, but the basic approach can be similar to the example just described.

In addition to a statistical profile of customer perceptions, it is a good idea to gather qualitative assessments from customers. Letters of complaint and praise can provide important clues to what employees are doing well and what they need to do better. According to Dick Scott, chief operating officer of Longs Drug Stores, "I'm getting letters like I haven't gotten in years. I'm getting more of them, and they're much more positive. They mention case after case where a Longs employee has gone way out of his or her way to do something special, and the customers appreciate it."

You might also want to interview individual customers now and then to find out in more depth how they feel and if their needs and desires are changing. *Critical incidents* that come up during such discussions can tell you a lot about how your customers are experiencing your service product.

Sometimes it's a good idea to use customer interviews as a way to validate your questionnaires. If you suspect a response bias in the questionnaire statistics, such as the possibility that the very happy or very disgruntled customers are responding more frequently than those who are basically satisfied, you can administer the questionnaire to a randomly selected group of customers in the form of an interview, in which the interviewer asks the questions and records the answers. Don't forget to test your questionnaire on a representative group of customers before you make it a permanent part of your SQMS. You'd be amazed how many people can misunderstand or misinterpret a question you consider perfectly clear.

It's not enough just to have a service quality measurement system; you have to put the information it provides to good use. Report the results in a simple, easy-to-digest form every month. Executive management should see the results, think about them, and discuss them. The agenda of the management meeting should include time to review and discuss the scores. And individual unit leaders can also receive the results and review them with the employees from time to time. Frontline employees are usually pleased and intrigued to have a chance to see how they and the company are doing. They take the results seriously and immediately begin to think about ways to do better.

If properly used, measurement and feedback do not punish people or make them feel guilty, even if the results show a need for significant improvement. The best approach is simply to present the results and say, "Here is what the customers are saying to us about the quality of our service. What are we going to do about this information?" This way the information serves a basic, matter-of-fact, business purpose. It becomes data for running the business, just like any other operational information.

INCENTIVES MUST POINT IN THE RIGHT DIRECTION

If you ask for A and yet you reward people for B, don't be surprised to get B, no matter how much you say you want A. Unless the organizational force-field—the perceived system of macro and micro rewards and sanctions that exerts pressure on the employees every hour of every day—points in the direction of service quality, you'll always be working uphill to try to make service quality a way of life. At every turn, the message will meet with contradictions. You may keep it alive and moving by the force of your determination, but until you deal with the infrastructural forces that *really* influence behavior, you will not have the basis of a permanent commitment to service.

There are several major things you can do to make sure the day-to-day incentive signals align with the philosophy of service quality.

Get rid of system craziness. As previously discussed, you must eliminate or restructure organizational processes that work against service quality. You must turn some of your sacred cows out to pasture and replace them with ones that support the mission. In some cases, you must work in the face of organizational traditions, values, and beliefs. Sometimes you have to find creative ways to accommodate tradition and honor existing values without letting them stand in the way of customer satisfaction.

Teach managers to appreciate their people.   Most working people are not all that bad; what most of them need and don't usually get is plain, down-to-earth appreciation for their work. If your managers are accustomed to dealing with them in strictly work-focused ways and only telling them when they've done something wrong, the workers will be going hungry most of the time. Teach your managers to "manage" less and lead more and to recognize that a big part of their job is to develop people, challenge them, inspire them, and—above all—appreciate them. This kind of leadership is much too rare in this Service Age, and it must become much more prevalent.

Set up a recognition process that honors excellence.   People need to know that giving their best energies in the name of customer satisfaction is worth something. Create a formal recognition system that puts people in the spotlight for doing something special for the customer. Consider material prizes or valuable rewards; greenbacks are a great form of feedback. There is nothing like seeing one of your peers receive a cash award or a prize of personal value to make it clear that management is serious about service. Rewards don't have to be lavish or expensive; the total cost of a recognition program is trivial compared to its impact.

Find and nurture your service heroes.   Identify the people who, day after day, time after time, do an exemplary job of dealing with their customers, either the external paying customers or the internal working customers. These are the people regarded by their peers as the embodiment of the belief in service excellence. Recruit them for the service quality task force. Form a group of them as a special advisory committee on service excellence. These are your water-walkers; the rest of the employees will look up to them and emulate them if they see that these people enjoy a special status as role models for service. In a number of top service companies, the chief executives honor service heroes who have been highly praised in customer letters by sending them personal letters of appreciation.

And finally, try in the long run to make the material reward systems in the organization align with the goal of service quality. Don't rush to tie the compensation system directly to service performance unless you are sure you have a fair and equitable basis for compensation and that some people won't be disenfranchised because their contributions are hard to measure. But eventually it makes sense to provide a system for promotion and advancement that favors people who make the most valuable contribution to the quality of the product and hence to the position of the company in its competitive environment.

CHAPTER 15

EXECUTIVE EVANGELISM

Success is never final.
—*J. W. Marriott, Sr.*

IT STARTS AT THE TOP

It is appropriate, in the final chapter of this book, to return to a fundamental precept I have stressed many times that never wears out from being mentioned too many times:

It starts at the top.

If there is one lesson I believe I have learned in observing and participating in major service quality programs and in discussing service with executives whose views I respect, it is that leadership is the crucial ingredient in achieving service excellence on the part of organizations. There needs to be an element of executive evangelism in operation; not only the chief executive but the other senior managers must preach, teach, and reinforce the gospel of service quality.

Employees, for the most part, want to do a good job; they want to give good service to their customers. If they're not doing it, more than likely something is standing in their way, and more than likely it's the organization. It's up to management to create the conditions that make service excellence possible and worthwhile. Employees will come through.

Executives who want to reach the levels of quality necessary to make service their competitive edge have to think carefully about the roles they are willing and able to play. Just as some employees find it easier than others to work in customer service jobs, so some executives find it easier than others to give the intensive, active, personal leadership their organizations will need. In this respect, the CEO becomes the strongest or weakest link in the chain of causality that leads to service quality. After all, service management is about *management*.

If the CEO is a presider, i.e., a relatively passive administrator who manages by the numbers, he or she may give the OK to a service quality program launched from somewhere down in the management structure, but the venture will never reach its full potential without the force of the top person's firm hand. It will probably always remain a program, even if it doesn't fade out.

But if the chief lives and breathes it, believes in it enough to become obsessed with it, and perceives it as nothing less than the basic competitive thrust for the organization's future, then sooner or later it will take hold and become part of the woodwork. People at the lower levels will begin to get the message: top management means business.

Jan Carlzon, president of SAS, had a challenge on his hands when he launched his major service initiative during a very difficult period when the company was taking a bath in red ink. He said to his executives and to his middle managers, "The first thing I have to do is convince you that I mean what I say: we're going to be in the service business." He set out to do that, and within approximately six months he had made his point with most of them. Similarly, the chief of any service organization has to establish personal credibility for the commitment to service quality. The other executives, the middle managers, the frontline supervisors, and the frontline employees have to believe he or she means business.

AN INTERVIEW WITH BILL MARRIOTT

I have met a number of chief executives who I believe carry within them the personal values and convictions necessary to lead their organizations to excellence in service. But of all of them, the name of J. Willard "Bill" Marriott, Jr., probably stands out as one of the legendary figures of the service revolution. In a time when many chief executives and senior managers are struggling with questions of strategy and trying to find promising futures for their organizations; in a time of doubt and concern about economics and markets; in a time of uncertainty and literal identity crises for many companies, it seems to me worthwhile to present some of the beliefs, convictions, values, and insights that a highly respected service executive like Bill Marriott has to offer.

I recently had the pleasure of spending some time with Bill Marriott, discussing his views on the management of service. Here is the substance of our conversation:

KA:

Your company, of course, is one of the legendary giants in the service business, and I think it would be helpful to other executives to know how you look at the business of service, and specifically how you manage it.

JWM:

You have to live it. It takes a total commitment. The CEO has to set an example for the rest of the organization, and he has to do whatever it takes to keep it uppermost in the minds of all the managers.

KA:

Specifically, how do you "live it"?

JWM:

Well, for one thing, I believe in going out into the organization and meeting as many people as I can and personally encouraging them. I spend probably 25 percent of my time traveling around to Marriott facilities and meeting the people. Last year I visited 100 hotels; I visited 50 restaurants; I visited 30 of our In-Flite kitchens that do airline catering. I'm on the road a tremendous amount because I believe that's part of my job.

KA:

So you believe in a very personal style of executive leadership?

JWM:

I do. People have to know you care about them. It has to be something you sincerely believe in. To do it and not be sincere about it is worse than not doing it.

KA:

I take it you became convinced of the value of personal leadership by working for your father?

JWM:

I was trained all my life by my father. He started the company in 1927 with the first A&W Root Beer stand in Washington. From the very beginning he was obsessed with quality and customer service. He was a perfectionist. Even in his later years, I can recall going with him to a board meeting. He'd be running late and he'd still stop and visit with the guy who was mopping the floor.

KA:

Was he a tough guy to work for?

JWM:

Yes, he was. As I said, he was a perfectionist. He was never satisfied with the status quo. He demanded a great deal of himself, and when I came into the business he demanded a great deal of me too. But people loved him. I can remember him getting letters from people who worked for him 30 years ago. They thanked him for what he had contributed to their lives.

KA:

He believed in a lot of personal contact, and apparently you do too?

JWM:

Lots of my contemporaries never mix with their people at all; they never walk into a kitchen or stop to shake hands with a front desk clerk. But I do. I think it's important. I just came back from London, where I visited one of our flight kitchens. I shook over 600 hands; everyone in the place. Now, I can't really tell you what that's worth. But it's enormously important, in my mind.

KA:

You feel it's important symbolically—the big boss visiting the people and letting them know that he knows they exist?

JWM:

It's an enormously symbolic act. In most companies, the employees don't even know what the top guy looks like. In this company, they recognize me when I come in the place. You saw what happened here; when I came into this hotel the first thing I did was shake hands and say hello to everybody at the front desk.

KA:

Sure, I could see how they reacted: "Gee, I just shook hands with Mr. Marriott."

JWM:

Right. As I say, I can't prove it really pays off, but I believe it does. Some of them don't know me; some of them probably don't care. You have to be prepared to take a little rejection along the way. But for most of them, it's an important personal experience.

KA:

Bill, how do you see your role as the chief executive? You've said you place a lot of importance on your symbolic role as a personal leader who is in contact with the people. What other aspects do you see?

JWM:

I see my role as that of a facilitator. A facilitator of management; a facilitator of teamwork; a facilitator of cooperation. I don't believe in the Harvard "book" manager. I don't believe in managing by the numbers. I think you have to go out there and get involved with the people and help them out.

KA:

Are you a perfectionist like your dad was?

JWM:

In some ways, yes. I've become a lot more tolerant as I've gotten older. My father was *really* a perfectionist. For example, he was a fanatic about mops and squirt cans. He was always checking the mop stations. He wanted the water to be clean and the mops not to be sour. His approach was one of constant little improvements. He was never satisfied; he could always find a way to do it a little bit better.

KA:

How would you say your style of management affects your subordinate managers?

JWM:

When I walk around and meet people, it lets the managers know that they can do it too. It tends to keep their energy up. I try to set an example for them.

KA:

Would you say the Marriott approach to management is rather informal, as opposed to authoritarian?

JWM:

We don't have any big shots around here. Guys come in who want to be big wheels, but they don't last; they don't get too far in the company, so they leave. We don't have any executive dining rooms or private elevators; I just don't believe in that stuff. It just isn't part of our culture.

KA:

Bill, how would you say you manage on a day-to-day basis? What kind of a boss are you?

JWM:

I believe in being respectful of people's time. I try to use power sparingly; I don't want a lot of people briefing me and catering to me all the time. I try to keep meetings short so they can get back to their work. I write a lot of memos to get the information I need for meetings, so we can get right down to business. But I think business can be fun too. I just came back from one of our facilities where I sat in on a staff meeting. Right in the middle of the meeting the secretary came in with 10 silver dollars and a game of Trivial Pursuit. They took a 10-minute break while everybody played Trivial Pursuit. Then they got back to the agenda. I thought it was a great idea. In fact, I won one of the silver dollars.

KA:

Bill, a lot has been made of Jan Carlzon's "great adventure" at SAS. What do you make of the SAS story?

JWM:

Well, Carlzon target-marketed the business traveler. He realized he had to have a hook of some kind, and in a falling market the business traveler was the one with the money. He came up with the right product and the right formula. If you want to look at a contrast, look at PeopleExpress. They tried the no-frills approach. They couldn't hold on to the business traveler, so they became the backpacker's airline; they couldn't survive.

KA:

It seems to me that none of the American airline companies is really in the service business today. What's your take on the state of service leadership in that industry?

JWM:

Well, C. R. Smith had it in spades at American. He developed a very strong cadre of service-minded managers. It started to fade after he left, but the ball kept rolling for quite a while. But I agree with you overall; no one in the industry is really making a splash with service.

KA:

Bill, one of the problems I think Carlzon faced at SAS, and is still facing so far as I can tell, was the classic middle management problem. He jumped over the middle managers and took the message straight to the frontline troops. That apparently caused a great deal of resentment on the part of the middle managers. What's your view on the so-called middle management problem today? Is it real, and what can we do about it?

JWM:

I think it *is* a problem. And I think Carlzon has a long road ahead of him. It's not easy. A lot of middle managers are in a state of confusion about what's expected of them. The middle manager has to understand what the company culture is. Most of them don't get enough training; the training they do get is more technical than emotional. I also think they need leaders to watch and learn from. It's important that their top managers lead by example and show them what's expected.

KA:

What do you think senior management can do to help middle managers get out of their role trap?

JWM:

Develop a strong team. The CEO needs to be a great listener; he has to participate in the process, but he has to build consensus. As I mentioned before, you have to be respectful of their time. As long as they're in the know and they're participating, they'll manage their people the same way. And I've said to our managers many times, "Take care of the people and they'll take care of your customers."

KA:

OK, Bill, here's a trick question for you. Most of the readers of this book won't be Bill Marriotts, who head up organizations that have two generations of history in service excellence. These people are trying to get their organizations to wake up and become service oriented. Could you step outside of your present situation and answer this: if you were to take over as the new chief executive of some other company which is not known for service, what steps would you take to get it there?

JWM:

Sure. The first thing I think I would do would be to assess the people I had to work with—the senior people. I'd find out which ones could make the commitment and which ones couldn't. I think you have to get rid of the square pegs, and then you start to work with the rest. Next, I think you have to get out and show them. Don't just sit in your office and talk about service; get out there and make it happen. You have to get the message out to the people. You saw what I did when I came into the management meeting today. I shook hands with every one of the managers I saw out in the reception area; you have to go to them. Then, you have to get them to set the standards and expectations for the employees. You can't just write it up in a book and send it out; it won't work. And you have to make it fun. Put some meaning into it.

KA:

And then?

JWM:

You just keep at it, that's all.

KA:

Just keep on keepin' on.

JWM:

Keep on keepin' on. My father always said, "Success is never final."
He believed it's harder to stay at the top than it is to get there.

KA:

OK, Bill, you fielded that trick question pretty well. Now, if you're
still patient with me, I'd like to ask you one more. The executives
and managers I'm writing this book for obviously aren't Bill Marriotts. They don't have the Bill Marriott personality. I can hear a
lot of them now, saying, "I don't have that kind of personality. I'm
not the kind of guy who goes around talking to people and shaking
their hands. I'm not the motivational type. That won't work for me."
How do you answer that? What about the guy who's not like you,
but who wants to give his organization the leadership it needs to be
in the service business?

JWM:

(laughing) Listen, *I'm* not that kind of a guy either. I'm not an
extrovert by nature. My father was. He was much more comfortable
than I am with meeting people and shaking hands. It doesn't come
easy for me at all. My idea of a good time is a nice fire and a good
book; maybe some good music. But I do it because I'm convinced
it works; because I enjoy the people and like to be with them.

KA:

How do you manage to do it if it doesn't come easy to you?

JWM:

Well, you just have to reach down inside yourself and find the
friendly, warm person. It's a psychic cost; no doubt about it. But
the rewards are tremendous. It works—I know that. And I can't
think of any more important contribution for the CEO to make.

KA:

Bill, thanks so much for your thoughts.

JWM:

You're most welcome.

REALISM, DETERMINATION, AND PATIENCE

By now, I hope we've debunked the mythology about quick fixes and instant success in service. It's a big job to teach the elephant to dance, turn the Queen Mary, get the ant army going in the same direction, or whatever your favorite metaphor suggests. Taking an organization from a so-so level of service to an excellent level of service involves work. It requires realism, determination, and patience on the part of senior management and on the part of the middle managers who have to make it work in the long run.

But it is possible. If it's possible in the world, then it's possible in your organization. It's a question of wanting to do it badly enough and being willing to go after it aggressively. And, in the long run, you have to "keep on keepin' on." Here's one of my favorite stories that illustrates the value of persistence.

A group of fraternity brothers were celebrating their 20th anniversary of graduating from the university. They had always been a small, tight-knit group, and 22 out of the 23 graduates showed up for the weekend celebration. As they were standing around the university club's boardroom, toasting one another's success and sporting their three-piece suits, Italian shoes, and Rolex watches, they noticed Hank was missing.

"Why do you suppose old Hank isn't here?" one asked. "Oh, you know Hank," somebody replied. "He was always kind of the black sheep of the group. He never did have a head for business. He probably didn't do too well and he just didn't feel good about showing up."

Just then somebody looked out the window and saw Hank getting out of a chauffeur-driven Rolls-Royce, attended by a platoon of aides. He came in to join the group.

One of the members said, "Gee, Hank, to tell you the truth, we never thought you'd show up. You were always a little slow in school, and we didn't think you'd really get far in business."

"Well, you know, you're right," Hank replied. "I never was too good at my courses, and I never had a head for figures. But I managed to find a product I could make for $1 and sell for $5. I did all right over the years; you know, it's really amazing how that 4 percent adds up."

So, part of success in service is just to keep on keepin' on.

SUCCESS IS NEVER FINAL

Service quality is like fitness; it doesn't last unless you keep at it. If you think all you have to do is write a check and give your OK to a service program and you'll be able to sit back and enjoy the fruits of service excellence forever, you're in for a big disappointment. The service commitment must be renewed every day. The quality of service in any organization will tend to regress to mediocrity unless it is actively and consciously managed.

I believe J. W. Marriott, Sr., was right when he said:

Success is never final.

You have to live it. You have to tend to it. You have to feed it, water it, care for it, care about it, and accept nothing less. In the Service Age, service is not just something managers should think about now and then; it *is* management.

INDEX